W9-BMU-860

The $100,000 Club

Other books by D. A. Benton

Lions Don't Need to Roar
How to Think Like a CEO

The $100,000 Club

How to Make a Six-Figure Income

D. A. Benton

WARNER BOOKS

A Time Warner Company

Warner Books, Inc., 1271 Avenue of the Americas,
New York, NY 10020
Visit our Web site at http://warnerbooks.com

 A Time Warner Company

First Printing: April 1998
10 9 8 7 6 5 4 3 2 1

Library of Congress Cataloging-in-Publication Data

Benton, D. A. (Debra A.)
The $100,000 club : how to make a six-figure income / D. A. Benton.
p. cm.
Includes index.
ISBN 0-446-52083-7
1. Finance, Personal. 2. Income. 3. Wealth. I. Title.
HG179.B418 1998
332.024'01—dc21 97-29934
CIP

Book design by Giorgetta Bell McRee

A special loving thanks goes to my parents, Fred and Teresa Benton. They provided balance in my early life, which enabled me to have the confidence to strike out into my own business at a young age.

My husband, Rodney Sweeney, the original mountain man, taught me more about life from nature than I learned from many years in business. As Voltaire wrote, "Man argues, nature acts."

To my associate Amy Williams, whose orientation to detail kept me striving for excellence in writing.

To my editor, Rick Wolff, whose guidance made this project easy to complete.

To my agent, Mike Cohn, whose wry sense of humor kept me entertained.

And to some very special friends: Nancy Albertini, Carol Ballock, Eunice Buhler, Mary Chung, Mindy Credi, Delores Doyle, Michelle Monfor Fitzhenry, Ernie Howell, Dr. Kelvin Kesler, and Pat Straley.

Debra Benton
Benton Management Resources
2221 West Lake Street
Fort Collins, CO 80521

Contents

The $100,000 Club

CHAPTER 1

Why $100K Can and Should Be Part of Your Career Plans

Are you being paid enough?

I suspect most people feel they need more money—not just to support their current lifestyle, but to provide for the one they aspire to.

Despite the risk of sounding politically incorrect: You want to make the big bucks! Although 91,993,582 households in this country earn around $31,241 a year—that's not the life for you.

Only 4 percent of U.S. households (approximately 4,035,799) earn *over* $100K. That sounds better, doesn't it? Seems like there must be room for a few more to make that money—to break that barrier and join the $100K Club—namely, *you*!

According to *Fortune,* "The new rule of thumb for being well-paid is to earn four times your age." Hey, it wasn't that long ago that *twice* your age meant well-paid! Regardless of any rule of thumb, the key is: What is the magic number for you?

Most everyone says $100K is a special number. Hence, *The $100K Club.* This book is to help you increase the odds of *your* becoming part of that group of four million earning that money.

But first, the myths and mistruths we were taught while growing up need to be corrected now that we're adults. They need to read:

- Money *is* an acceptable topic of conversation.
- Money *does* buy happiness.
- Money *does* make the world go 'round.
- Money is *not* the root of all evil.
- Do what you love and money will follow *only* if others love it too.
- If you have health, kindness, balance, and money, you *do* have everything.
- Both smart *and* dumb can earn big money.
- Rich people are *not* bad people.
- People who say they *don't* care about money either don't have enough or have too much.

There is a spiritual snobbery some people take on about money. To say you don't like money would be to not like nearly *anything*—because money supplies nearly everything.

Man was born to grow rich by using God-given abilities: intelligence, thoroughness, right reasoning, promptness, tenacity, patience, labor. (When Moses came down from the mountain, he did not bring the commandment "Thou shalt not make money.")

By using your abilities and making money, you give yourself power, leisure, solitude, and liberty.

To read this book about making $100K (and more) is *not* to learn about greed or to become a soulless, covetous money monger. It's about choices, discipline, values, relationships, and self-esteem.

(By the way, it's okay to be greedy with new ideas for growth. That's what this book is about. One resulting benefit is money.)

It is true that money carries an assortment of distinct and powerful emotions for people, both good and bad. But that does not negate its role as a basic, important, and understandable system of communication. For better or worse, money is the resource, now and in the future, that ties society together.

You can choose to spend it, save it, or share it—but first you have to get it.

Aside from those born with an inheritance already in the bank, the rest of us have to be born with *desire.* Desire to learn. Desire to work. Desire to sweat. Desire to have someone say about you someday, "Look, now there's a successful person."

Being a successful person can mean lots of different things, of course, but here I mean financial, emotional, and intellectual—*balanced success.*

Salary, or income, is an extremely confidential subject in this country. It is not socially acceptable to brag (or even tell) people how much you make. A Procter &

Gamble alum told me, "You could get fired if you told someone how much you make at the company."

The $100K Club is all about that private subject. I have written about what people do write home to Mom about: moving to a window corner office, getting a premium company car, their own key to the washroom, a wooden desk instead of a metal one, the title of vice president, et cetera. *And* what they *should* write home about—making $100K plus.

But first, can you think back to your first awareness of money?

One man answered that question, "As a kid I lived in California and my dad and I would drive through Beverly Hills. He would point toward wealthy people's homes and tell me, 'Thieves live there.' That's how I viewed people with money."

A female business owner answered, "As I was growing up, my aunt used to say to me, 'It's just as easy to fall in love with a rich person as a poor one, so be careful who you choose to go out with. . . . But always carry a quarter in your bra so you have money to make a telephone call if you need to get away from someone.' "

A man who has been included in the *Forbes* list of the world's wealthiest people said, "As a child I saw a television special about the Rothschilds and decided I wanted to be like them. It feels very appropriate."

A wealthy friend surprised me by saying, "When I was six years old, I asked my folks for an Oh Henry! candy bar for Christmas. They said they couldn't afford it. Right then I vowed to be able to afford as many as I wanted when I grew up." (He said this to me as we stopped at a convenience store for gas and he purchased six Oh Henry! bars. He didn't eat any, he just bought them.)

So pause here a moment and try to think back to your early awareness about money. Why? Because we all have experiences that form our unconscious attitude about the almighty dollar. Sentiments that as adults can cause problems in accomplishing monetary goals.

We all have attitudes formed in our childhood about relationships with most everything in life: the opposite sex, food, beauty, religion, money. You name it and a view was formed by individual upbringing. Regardless of the subject, it's an outlook you can change with your own free will.

You need to take a proactive look at yourself and your past as it relates to money. Psychologists popularly label this "fear of success versus fear of failure." I prefer to just recognize that we all have relationships regarding money that stem from various experiences, both good and bad. It's our choice to bemoan the fact that our rearing causes fear of success (or failure). *Or* it's our choice to recognize that possibility and decide now, as a thinking person, to change any prohibitive attitudes.

You might say, "Well, that will require therapy!" If you choose to go that route, you will spend money to get someone to help you alter your thinking. Or you can do like many who do well do and sort out the reasoning yourself. It requires only two things: recognition, then change. As the Nike advertisements say, "Just do it."

Some might say, "Well, I can't change those deeply embedded experiences." True, you can't change the experiences, but you can change your perspective about them. You, and only you, can decide to take on new views that support your goals, give you and your family new training, and conquer any self-imposed limitations rooting around in your psyche.

(Just one example of a self-limiting attitude is the currently used business buzzword *FUD*. It's an acronym for "Fear, Uncertainty, and Doubt." It relates to any daring decision you need to make. FUD is something you can reverse. Perhaps substitute "First Undo Derogatory" when you use FUD as a step to changing.)

A company has to change to progress and stay competitive. That might mean altering attitudes toward its past. When businesses do it, they call it changing the "corporate culture." If an organization of hundreds, even thousands, can transform a corporate mentality, then an individual surely can.

J. R. Simplot founded his potato-based agricultural empire in the 1920s. (His company supplies McDonald's with 50 percent of its french fries.) Now he is emerging as one of the biggest players in the semiconductor technology world. He follows only Bill Gates and Paul Allen in a mind-boggling ballooning of his financial worth. According to *Fortune,* "The man makes a fortune in the era of Manifest Destiny and then makes another in the age of the Internet. It seems impossible." Imagine the transformation he's gone through: As he puts it, he started his company before the typewriter, much less the computer!

Change Any Limiting Attitudes You Might Have Toward Making the Big Money

People *can* change. Of course, when they say and *think* they can't, then they can't. If they think they can, they can. (You already know that to be true; I'm just reminding you about self-imposed mental blocks.)

If, in your self-reflection, you discover negative blocks about making lots of money—get over it! Switch that thought now. If you don't, in five, ten, twenty years you will kick yourself in the underalls for not overturning it.

The business world has undergone revolutionary change and there really aren't the limitations there might have been at one time. You have to realize that and not stay stuck in the "this can't be done by me" mind-set. My professional and personal experience of having worked with many $100K members is that making money, beyond the level needed to satisfy basic needs, is, interestingly, about self-respect.

If, by the way, you think that in order to make $100K you have to be a thief, be neurotic, be a workaholic, or sell yourself out—well, you are dead wrong.

There are many good, well-liked people who make big money and are still good and well-liked. Country Music Association performer of the year Reba McEntire is a down-home entertainer who's adored, admired, and respected by her fans and peers alike. She unashamedly says she works all-out to earn all the money she possibly can.

Parishioners and fellow clergy in San Diego call Father Joe Carroll the "hustler priest." Not because he gets paid so much, but because he raised a record $11.7 million for a homeless shelter. Few would say he lacks ethics, despite the huge money he's involved with.

The list of 100K people who lead balanced lives and are honest, sane, hardworking, and deserving of their wages is longer than the list of those who aren't. The bad ones get the publicity and notoriety, thus giving a sordid reputation to wealth. That is *good* because it reminds clean players to stay clean while weeding out the losers.

Wealth, in and of itself, is not bad. What it can cause you to do can be bad or good. I prefer to think my readers use it for good. Some won't, though, and I apologize to mankind for that. But the mission in *The $100K Club* is to help the majority who desire and deserve to earn much more than they are currently earning.

To make $100K you have to decide to do some fairly simple things *well* and *consistently.* This book is about those specific things. But it isn't just about making big money; it's about becoming a person who deserves big money and takes the responsibility for getting it.

Your very being consists of your imagination of yourself. Your monetary goals revolve around what you'll cause yourself to do, both in big and small ways.

That lesson was reinforced for me recently when I left town for a three-day speaking trip.

As I buckled the airplane seat belt, I reached for my briefcase to get out some work. The spot where I keep my wallet was empty. I had left it on my office desk. I didn't have a single credit card to use on the airplane telephone to call for money. I didn't have *any* currency, not even pocket change. Nothing. Despite what my W-2 tax form reads, at that moment I had zero money. I thought through my dilemma and knew I could get money once at my destination, but I had to get there *first*—and I couldn't even pay for a taxi to the hotel! (I checked in the brochure: no free shuttle service to the hotel.)

I always carry with me in my briefcase a copy of one of the books I've written. It makes for fun conversation on an airplane when I can subtly show (er, show off) the book to my seatmate. The desperate thought crossed my mind, *I have to sell this book on this plane to get some money to pay for the taxi.* (It seemed like a better option than begging for a handout or pawning my watch.)

Since I'd been upgraded to first class, there was only one seatmate. I bemoaned the fact that if I had stayed in coach and gotten a center seat, I'd have had two people to try to sell the book to, thus increasing my odds.

So I started mentally planning. First, size up the situation—namely, the buying potential of this one seatmate. He was dressed in khakis, was sockless, and wore a monogrammed crew shirt. My first thought: *Oh great, a trust-fund baby!* But I patiently listened and carefully observed. He started talking to a pretty woman sitting across the aisle. Turned out she worked for him. Good. At least he was in business. But I couldn't look too eager or brash. So I waited.

The airplane flight pattern that day coincidentally took us directly over the isolated Colorado mountain valley where my husband and I live in a log cabin. I casually looked out the window and commented, "See that open spot? That's where I live." (You have to admit, it's an original opening line.)

"Really?" was his less than impressed response. He turned back to the pretty woman.

As he took a sip of his orange juice, I initiated some more conversation: "I couldn't help but overhear you talking. Are you in the beverage distribution business?"

"We're a beer distributor," he said.

"Oh, I see. You were using business terms I hear with one of my clients, Pepsi-Cola. That's why I asked." (Notice how I slipped in the information that I was in a business where I have big-name clients like Pepsi-Cola?)

Fortunately, some level of curiosity caused him to ask, "What kind of business are you in?"

"I'm a consultant and an author of business books," I answered. But I still wasn't sure what his job was and whether he would have any interest in buying my book. So I offered, "I notice you and she"—I pointed to the woman across the aisle—"are talking. Would you like to sit together? I can move if you need to discuss business." I was taking a risk of losing my book buyer, but again, I couldn't look too eager about engaging in conversation with him.

"No, we'll be together the rest of the trip." He added so she could hear, "She's the top manager in my company." Then kiddingly, "I see enough of her."

Great! I thought. *He practices what I preach about professional effectiveness: building subordinates' self-esteem, using humor, being pleasantly assertive.* My stuff would be like preaching to the choir, as they say.

So I casually commented in a quiet voice, "What you just did—praising her—is part of what I write about in my books."

The compliment intrigued him enough to ask, "Would I have heard of any of your books?"

"Perhaps. *Lions Don't Need to Roar* or *How to Think Like a CEO,*" I told him.

"Sure I have. I saw an article on that *Lions* book. Is it available at most bookstores?" he asked with some genuine interest.

"Yes, anywhere in the country." Then—without a frantic tone—I added, "If you are interested, I happen to have a copy with me. If you want to buy it, I'd be glad to autograph it for you."

"Great. How much is it?" he asked, reaching for his wallet.

When I put his twenty-dollar bill in my briefcase, I fondled it for a few seconds. After not having any money, it sure felt good between my fingers. Then I selected a specifically secure pocket in the briefcase to guarantee no mishap of losing it. I was *rich*!

I felt like an honored member of the $100K Club with that twenty dollars! It was a feeling of pure happiness.

I hope *you* frequently experience that happiness on a much grander scale. With that wish, I make this announcement:

THE $100K CLUB IS OPEN TO NEW MEMBERS!

The requirements? As I mentioned before, there are several simple things you need to do well and consistently. Here's one of those simple things: You must be willing to add to your self-worth *every* day.

While adding to your self-worth typically means making money, in the financial sense it can also mean investing money, learning a timely job skill, developing a new personality trait, solving a time-consuming energy-draining problem, controlling time, managing an attitude, improving appearances, even building muscle.

Adding to your self-worth will make you more valuable monetarily, professionally, mentally, physically, emotionally. That's successful living. That's a $100K Club member.

Regardless of the exact dollar figure that lights up their eyes—six figures, seven, even eight figures—a lot more will try than succeed. If you want to be the one who succeeds, this book is for you.

I've spent the last twenty years around people whose financial earnings put them into $100K and far beyond. I've studied, watched, interviewed, and consulted for them. What I've learned, from those who have made it, is yours for the taking. As I stated earlier, one of the simple requirements is to—*every* day—add to your self-worth.

I have a friend with a trademark greeting: When asked "How's it going?" he answers, "Spectacular . . . but getting better." People always know he will say it and they ask all the time just to hear his enthusiasm again.

Of course, he has to walk the walk. Like the day I called him and he informed me that the company he'd worked for the last twenty of his sixty-one years had been sold and he and everyone in the office would be terminated. At that exact moment he was missing an important meeting that could have meant a new job, but because the bank next door had been robbed and his front-office door was bolted by the police and the parking lot was blocked off, he couldn't leave.

"I'm rather excited, though, even at my age. I have two house payments, two car payments, and one motor-home payment. But I refuse to allow myself a pouting party. You know me: If I don't learn something new every day, I'm sliding backward. . . . By the way, do you know what *et. seq.* means?"

"No, I don't," I answered. "Why do you ask?"

"Well, it keeps coming up in the real estate law classes I'm teaching and I don't know what it means, so today I'm going to find out," he told me.*

Another acquaintance of mine is a female business leader who says it's her personal mission to add to her worth every day. She's forty-one years old but looks thirty-two because she takes good care of herself so that her body will hold up for all the work she puts it through. She says, "I have to 'win' every day. That means I'm either in a race or in a battle."

She watches ESPN every evening. It doesn't matter the sport; she just likes to study the competition. She says, "Win, win, win, that's what I want. I analyze individual players, the depth of the team, the defense, who's on the bench. Everything I'm interested in is based around winning and losing, because that's what I deal with every day in the marketplace.

*He wrote me a note the next day and explained that in Latin *et. seq.* means "in sequence or logically following." Another example of walking the walk by following through with that day's objective.

"*Every* day I read a story or part of a book about [athletic] coaches. I learn so much from them. I'm reading something by Don Shula now, but Vince Lombardi was my favorite. I feel I missed something in my life not knowing him. . . . Last night I read an article about a marathon runner who pushes his brother, who has cerebral palsy, in a three-wheeler during training runs. It brought tears to my eyes. When you ignite the human spirit like that, you have so much energy to burn."

Then you have the energy to make significant money!

All $100K Club members add to their self-worth every day *before* they make the big money. The habit isn't formed once you reach some financial goal; it's to get you *to* that financial goal and to keep you at and beyond that level.

Fortunately, there are myriad ways for you to add value to yourself on a daily basis so that you are worthy of earning six figures. That is also what this book is about: being worthy of big money as a reflection of your mental creativity, intelligence, and drive.

In the 1980s making money was the goal in itself: having more showpieces, cars, clothes, or someone on your arm. Not today.

In the 1990s and beyond, instead of having more things, *do* more things. Be the master of your own fate. Be the superhero you (and your family) look up to in your life.

An old study concluded that men view money as adding to their power and women view money as adding to their freedom. Today the thinking has to be: Combine power and freedom in the limited time available.

People who are successful do what's required seven days a week. It's not just work, it's fulfilling their own dream.

You don't need to do it like anyone else. But if you're like most who have made it already, you want to know what others have experienced. Then you can pick your own route.

To help you do that, the chapters in this book are laid out as follows:

Chapter 2 is about following your heart and soul to make a six-figure income. The fact is that you will be spending a great deal of your life working at it, so you had better enjoy yourself. If you chase the bucks too hard but lose yourself in the process, not only will you be unhappy but you might get fired. We want to make sure that doesn't happen.

We all know that corporate executives can make six-, seven-, eight-figure salaries—but what other kinds of jobs do too? Yes, some artists, rodeo cowboys, manufacturers' reps, pilots, and long-distance truckers do also. But in all fields, a lot more people enter a field than excel in it. The third chapter explains what makes the difference between the two.

If a corporate job is your chosen route, then you want to get yourself in the right position to get those high-paying jobs. Chapter 4 will reveal how to set yourself apart from the competition. And—very important—what can be done to get over the hurdle when you're stuck at a certain money level.

Chapter 5 provides fresh thinking on how to job hunt at the $100K level. The people who do the screening of résumés and the interviewing will tell you exactly what they do and don't like.

If you develop a niche and are able to work out of your home, how do you compete with the big boys with deep pockets, use the government as a partner, stay motivated, and reenter the corporate world if necessary? Telecommuters will want to pay particular attention to Chapter 6.

Chapter 7 is about trade-offs and the decision whether the sacrifices are worth it to you. It's an upbeat, real-world view of what big money does and doesn't mean.

And finally, Chapter 8 is a 20-point checklist designed for you to rate yourself, both for where you are now and for in the future, on your chance of success in joining the $100K Club.

There is a lot of conventional wisdom about making money that isn't very wise. There are many myths about what making big dollars means. A lot is misunderstood. *The $100K Club* changes that.

As National Finals Rodeo bull-rising champion (and $100K Club member) Tuff Hedeman says, "In order to ride bulls, you really have to focus and concentrate on what it takes to make a good ride."

That's what we are going to concentrate on: making "a good ride" with the bulls in business. The good thing is that you don't have the physical pain or the eight-second time limit to contend with—like Tuff Hedeman does in his work!

If you've been working toward this goal casually, then take this advice and go all-out for it.

When you have a tough day (which we all do) and it's a bit depressing, discouraging, or disappointing, take one hour off and do one of the following:

- Visit the hospital where you want to donate money for a wing named after your father.
- Write out a check to your favorite charity (no, not to yourself) with a note that reads, "More will follow."
- Go to a car dealership and test-drive some racy new model.
- Sit down at the computer with your son or daughter and use the Internet to review the pros and cons of selected schools he or she wants to attend.
- Leave a supportive, loving (surprise) message on your partner's voice mail, just to display your affection and appreciation.
- Seek out the person on the front page of the business section who achieved some big goal and congratulate him by telephone or with a handwritten note.

Then go back to whatever task you were doing before your one-hour sabbatical. The brief break refreshes you, improves your perspective, and rewards you for your diligence.

When it is all over in your life, you want to be able to

say to yourself something like GOP Senator Arlen Specter says (on his aborted campaign for president): "I would have kicked myself in the ass if I hadn't tried."

I'll close this chapter with one of my definitions of pure happiness. *The period of time when you are on the verge of making big money, with the real possibility that it will happen.*

My hope for you is that this book in your hands will give you the tools to experience that pure happiness.

"My advice is to select an endeavor you truly love. You'll be more inclined to put in the effort necessary to achieve success. Countless individuals have selected a profession because it appears lucrative. It isn't until they become fully immersed that they find out that it is something they do not enjoy and, as a consequence, do not give it justice.

"Also, it is important to always keep in mind the commitment required to achieve your goals. All too often an individual will attain a measure of success, feel that they have made it, and lose the edge. It is like a marathon runner who reaches the front of the pack: They must still maintain the same pace to remain in the lead."

—PETER MACKINS,
CPA, The Fielding Institute

"You must be driven to do something you love with a passion, get into that field on the bottom, swallow your pride as you learn, and listen and benefit from every mistake. An attitude of perseverance and patience is an absolute necessity."

—DENNIS HOPPE,
President, Hoppe
Management Concepts, Inc.

"Focus on what you want to do for a career first before focusing on what you will earn. Almost any career path you choose has the potential to provide a six-figure income. The most important thing is to choose a career that fits within your skill set and involves doing things that you enjoy. Focus on doing your best, getting to know people who are successful within your career choice, learning the skills and the success measures required to be the best performer, and doing it better than anyone else. You'll have a much greater chance of achieving a six-figure income living out your dreams versus fighting through a drudgery."

—Brad Williams,
President, Dakota Beverage

"Develop a strong personal ethic that includes working hard and then working smart; commit to success but not at the expense of fairness; educate yourself beyond conventional means for exceptional results; what you expect of yourself will be closely linked to what you accomplish. In the end there is absolutely no substitute for being in the right place at the right time—so be in a lot of places."

—E. A. "Butch" Teppe,
Vice President, Victor L.
Phillips Co.

CHAPTER 2

The Key to a Six-Figure Income: Follow Your Heart and Soul

On Christmas Eve I went into a 7-Eleven store to pay for gasoline. The man in line ahead of me approached the clerk and pointed to the lottery scratch-game cards on display under the counter and said, "Give me one of each of them."

"All ten games?" the female clerk asked.

"Yes." He paid for them, picked them up off the counter, and immediately handed them back to the clerk. "Merry Christmas. These are yours to scratch," he said a little shyly as he turned to leave.

He was almost through the door when she called out, "Do you want to come over to my house tomorrow and help me scratch them?"

With a surprised but happy face he said, "Sure."

Now, you can't tell me money doesn't buy happiness when you follow your heart!

Of all the excuses people use for not going after six-figure incomes, the most prevalent one is, "Money won't buy me happiness." You're right, but then again, neither will poverty.

A balanced* life gives you happiness . . . and money is part of that balance. Just as money is part of quality of life. So is work. So are family, community, health, achievement, and all other aspects of living that are valuable to you.

It's important to note that money *can* be a part of a well-rounded life—and that can mean six-figure money.

People mistakenly sell themselves on the singular notion: Do what you love and money will follow. It's too simple an idea. If you love being a kindergarten teacher, a policeman, or a military officer, that is great. Doing the work because you love it is fine. But don't count on big money to follow. Your income will be largely psychological.

If your thinking is one-dimensional—"I just want to do what I love. I don't want money"—you will severely limit the potential for a truly balanced life. Remember, I included money as part of the balance. In today's society, you are missing out if you don't include money also.

*I use the word *balance* because it is popularly understood. A better word is *congruence. Balance* implies giving exact attention to all elements; *congruence* implies a relative weighing of elements. Use the one that fits you best.

My friend, fellow author, and consultant Jack Falvey says, "Balance in life is admirable but not necessary. In fact, a healthy imbalance or positive obsessiveness can produce very worthwhile results."

In our parents' time the choice was work hard to make money *or* love what you do to enjoy life. Today you can do it differently than it's ever been done before. You can and must have it *both* ways to have it at all.

Having money and happiness is becoming less of a rarity. It is the realistic, modern ideal to strive for.

Former New York police officer John Bianchi made custom leather holsters on his days off. Over a period of years his hobby business went on to become the largest manufacturer of holsters and belts for police officers and the military worldwide.

Military officers Colin Powell, Norman Schwarzkopf, and even Scott O'Grady (the captain whose plane was shot down by the Serbs and who survived by wits and eating bugs) turned into six-figure-income earners with book writing, speeches, and movie deals.

Berry Fowler was a junior high school teacher who saw parents pay for their children to receive private coaching in math and reading, so he founded Sylvan Learning Systems to provide after-school tutoring. Seven years later he sold the 118 franchises he'd built up for $5.2 million.

Although teaching, law enforcement, and the military don't normally mean six-figure incomes—with the right stuff happening, they can.

Like most things, the earlier you work on the "ideal," the greater your chance of getting it. Starting on it early (or at least at this time) won't absolutely guarantee you'll make your target, but *not* starting on it now does guarantee you won't make it.

YOU CAN HAVE IT *ALL**

Be prepared, though, for the fact that a balanced (congruent) life, as I write of it, takes a lot of effort. For example, earning big bucks in your lifetime and having a satisfying personal life will take a lot out of you. Make sure the effort expended is worth it: Follow your heart. Like comedian Tim Allen says, "All the energy it took to get here, I don't think I'll have it again."

Beginning now, don't waste any more time or energy not using your *all* in pursuit of big bucks. What do I mean? Set your mind to having it all—which means whatever is *all* to you. *All* can be family, health, children, friends, recreation, service, integrity, security, home, making a difference, and personal growth, both spiritual and financial.

All is important. You can't be a happy $100K Club member if you aren't healthy. (Your daily do list must include exercise.) You can't be a $100K Club member if you are in debt. (If you can't afford to lose your job, you won't be able to stand up to wrong and bad things that happen in business.)

There are as many different people as there are different ways of living a dream. What motivates a research-

**All* means integrating everything in life important and interesting to you, both financially and emotionally. It means nothing is left out when considering how you spend your existence. It means doing more of what you want, all of the time, than others are probably doing.

and-development person may not do the same for the salesperson. When the salesperson might want instant gratification of a done deal, for example, the R&D person wants a discovery. Everyone's all is different. The important thing is to find out yours.

Here's part of the all for one of the wealthiest men in New York, Donald Trump: "Everyone asks what drives me. The money? It's really not. It's the aesthetics. I love the aesthetics so much that I fight hard on other things to get 'em. That includes everything that goes into a deal. I love creating beautiful things. And this"—he gestures across the city before him—"this is my canvas."

Part of the all for comedian Drew Carey is humorously expressed: "I like to run stop signs in the rain just to make the cops stand out in it to give me a ticket. I can pay for it. Why make money if you can't enjoy it? When the cop asks, 'Know why I stopped you?' I say, 'Yeah. Know why I ran the stop sign?' "

Now, I realize Carey's words are a little outlandish when talking balance of life. But for his personality, that is possibly a part of his quality of life . . . part of his all.

You need to first stop and think about what makes up your all. Honestly ask yourself if what you're doing fulfills your all, consider what you need to change (what's lacking), and do something about it. Scrutinize and synchronize what's valuable to you.

The more you can clearly pinpoint what you need and want in personal and professional fulfillment, the easier it is to achieve. People don't fail because of skill level. They fail because of fit. They don't fit all their interests into one package—including their money interest.

As one female CEO said to me about her all, "There is nothing wrong with people at my church knowing what I do for a living. It's okay to combine those interests."

It's a matter of desire, like I wrote about in Chapter 1. If you desire balance, it's worth working to achieve it. Why work and earn anything at all otherwise? If you forget to live, why bother?

Pueblo Indians were traditionally taught as children that when they went to work among the corn and other plants, they should sing, because if they didn't have good thoughts and a good heart, the plants would not grow well and the tribe would not get a good harvest as a result.

Metaphorically speaking, I hope you are singing in your heart, every day, at your tasks.

As some sage philosopher once wrote, "Every man dies. Not every man lives."

When I talked with $100K Club members about loving their work, I learned something very interesting. Unless you know and work on your alls, not a lot of money will stay with you even after you earn it! If people don't enjoy how they make their money, they can't seem to keep it. They lose it.

Get It Together Inside Your Head

You absolutely must be happy first, before you earn big money. People are happy when they balance their alls. If you are not contented with life in general, no amount of money will buy you pleasure. Likewise, having world peace, a healthy economy, well-mannered children, a paid mortgage, and vacations in Aspen doesn't all make for glee. If you don't have it inside now, none of those things—including money—will give you that.

Geoff is a friend of mine who recently resigned from a Fortune 100 company to buy a franchise organization in which he is his own boss. Even his wife gets to work with him in his new venture. "I'm making less money than I was and less than my friends, but I am enjoying what I do now more than at any time in my life. What is particularly satisfying is that I had this as part of my plan for the last six years, and it finally happened."

What people mean when they proclaim "Money won't buy happiness" is exactly that. They don't mean you can't be happy with money. There is a big difference. If you aren't a generally happy person while working for the six-figure goal, you will, first, likely not get it, or second, not enjoy it if you do get it.

Inner happiness comes from:

- How much we enjoy what we have
- How we meet the events in life

- Who is happy around and with us
- The satisfaction from enjoying personal connections with others
- Increased confidence
- Attained goals
- Having what we like, not what others think desirable
- Thinking interesting thoughts
- The ability and desire to be kind
- Control we exert in our life
- The challenge of work: That's living your all

If you aren't content with what you have, you won't be content with getting more of it. But you don't have to be content with where you are. Contentment won't improve your position in life if it causes you to stop stretching. Just don't confuse who you are with what you are and what you have.

An interesting thing about pure happiness: If you find it in *some* things, it becomes easier to find in a lot of other things too.

Don't let one aspect of your all become a larger piece of your life than it needs to be. Take your job, for instance: If the job alone becomes your all, it leaves you no opportunity for release and growth.

Don't Delay the Discovery and Determination of Your Alls

The early years of a career are the toughest time to maintain balance. When you are young you have lots of unfocused energy, are typically single, without children and the various "tugs" at your time. And worst of all, there isn't a clear picture of your alls.

Determining what does and doesn't work for you, in making yourself a well-rounded person, takes lots of testing, guessing, and retrying. If you don't start this trial-and-error process early in a career, you may regret it in your later years.

But suppose you did not go through this soul-searching and you are making big money anyway? The advantage you have is that you can use the money to help determine your all now!

I would hope that you do *not* experience financial success before inner togetherness. You might just stick it out and endure imbalance in your life if you get big money early; it's a form of golden handcuffs. The joy that will come to you from making six figures will cloud the not-yet-personally-together mental side and thwart individual development. Far better to get it together first and then get the money. But don't wait too long! Go after balance like it's a horse that has to be roped before it gets away.

People who don't aggressively pursue a well-rounded life end up in news articles describing people with high-flying positions quitting to spend time with their family. Trouble is, it is already their third family because they've spent numerous years *not* scrutinizing and synchronizing their alls when they should have.

To compound the problem, it is often downsizing, global competition, demands from boards, and increased office pressures that finally force people to look to their personal life. Unfortunately that can be too late.

Regardless of our great plans, we all have stressful surprises in our life—the death of a family member, birth of a child, divorce, physical illness, failure to get ahead, loss of a job, a natural disaster—that understandably derail us temporarily. Interruptions have to be factored in when you are looking at all aspects of your life. If some thought goes into obstacles before they occur, the surprise can be minimized and the response will be more effective.

There are few reasons that justify long-term, real, personal unhappiness for people living in the United States in this day and age—except self-imposed misery. It goes back to upbringing and how you choose to deal with things. Regardless of the experience, you can choose to be happy *this* day.

I think about one female company president who said to me, "I grew up in the projects. By the time I turned eighteen I was supporting myself and my family by taking in laundry, cleaning houses, even picking cotton. It was also at age eighteen that I decided: I always want to be happy. That was my goal. Twenty-two years later I still am."

If people with harder lives then most of us have experienced can do it, well then so can we.

Bob Berkowitz has had a media career to envy: reporter at CNN, ABC, and NBC; White House correspondent; and host of his own internationally syndicated talk show. Success comes to him because he knows his alls. "I will not do anything I don't love, believe in, am proud of, have fun at, look forward to, and go to bed happy about what I did that day."

Don't sacrifice value and character for earning money, but don't mistakenly think you can't have both money and values.

People spend their whole lives looking for shortcuts. There are none. If you follow your heart, you will discover fun ways to make the exertion *feel* like a shortcut. But the reality is that you have to work at finding that equilibrium among all of your alls.

When Jack, a CEO, was a child, he was frequently told by adults: "Jack, you could do so much more if you focused on one thing instead of so many things."

As an adult he admits he still doesn't focus on one thing: He has all kinds of interests and he pursues them. As he says, "I use up my interest in an area, then go on to another. That's how I keep balance in my professional life today."

He continues:

> I have a group of [company] president friends and we've been together for thirty years. We

went through problems together, divorces, thefts, but it was never a cookie-cutter group by any means.

Out of the forty [in this group], there are three or four pushing just as hard as they were thirty years ago. But the rest are shallow, lonely, and at loose ends. They all have big money, but some have lost their businesses, some sold them, some have had them bought out from under them. These are people who never spent time on interests other than their business.

When you ask what they are doing now, you can see them physically shrink. They have no company and no job to report on and they are lost.

They really don't have a partnership marriage. They take up golf to fill the void. They don't want to start over. They don't want to be bad at something. Don't want to go through that again. They have lots of "would'ves, could'ves, and should'ves."

Myself, I'm not looking for things to do as much as trying to find enough time to do all the things I want.

What Jack and others like him have discovered is that you must put equilibrium into your daily life. No one else will try to help give you any balance. It is up to you. If anything, many will try to throw you off by pushing their wants and needs. Obviously, priorities need to be set, but proportion is also a priority.

Bill Coors, head of the Coors beer company, addressed a high school graduating class with a caution that money does not mean happiness. He said most of the people he associates with have made vast amounts of money and aren't happy. His warning was not meant to dissuade the graduates from financial success. His message was: Jointly make money *along with* being true to yourself.

Unfortunately, there are far too many rich, unhappy people out there: three and four marriages down the drain, their kids on serious drugs, personal security problems, huge tax liabilities, multiple mortgages, constant keeping up with the Joneses, ulcers, and stress, to name just a few of their problems. These people set bad examples to aspiring $100K Club members. It's important to note: Those same people would be miserable without money also. Don't join their ranks.

For some reason, no formal schooling ever attempts to help us explain or understand the sources of our own well-being. To remedy the situation, here's help to understand options and structure choices—before, during, and after you make the big bucks:

- Clearly know the things that make up *your* all; work at work that interests you.
- Work with intensity; have targets and have measures.
- Maintain a level of fun at all times, even when it isn't.

- Have faith in yourself so you'll take necessary plunges.
- Get along with people.

Clearly Know the Things that Make Up Your *All*

Appreciate the fact that those ideas might have been instilled by upbringing; but as an adult, you pick and choose the ones that fit your makeup *today.* Accept the fact that others will criticize, chide, dismiss, disapprove of, or attack your choices. Let them. You need to be complete unto yourself. Strong people make their own way. As long as the whole package fits you, it will turn out fine.

Set aside a special day to do this. Go to the sea, the mountains, or the prairie. Sit and listen, observe, smell, and think. You can't do this as effectively in a city; you can't block out all the trash.

First, make up your mind where you want to go and what you want to do. Remember to consider: Can you truly make money at this or is it a nonearning occupation?

Remind yourself of your alls, first thing every morning and fifteen times a day.

Conduct a self-analysis during happy times as well as not-so-happy times for a more objective outcome.

The questions a headhunter asks you during a job search are the same questions you should ask yourself:

- What have I enjoyed most about my jobs?
- What do I do in my free time?
- Where do I see myself five or ten years from now?
- What kind of company do I like to work for?
- Who has been the best person I've worked for?
- What interests my family?

Take the last question, for example: If you are attached to a significant other, his or her all has to be a part of yours also. You should know your partner's fears, likes, and dislikes about things in general and about your six-figure income climb in particular. Be concerned with his or her welfare in this whole plan.

In short, if you don't keep a proportioned balance—between family, friends, business, religion, health, and hobbies—making $100K or more will be a meaningless chore.

It happens all the time: An engineer in North Carolina willingly accepts a job with a 25 percent pay decrease just to move back to Iowa, where his three children and grandchildren live. A White House official leaves a promising post to allow more time with his son. A Fortune 100 CEO resigns to spend more time with his family. An eighty-hour-per-week Realtor quits to save her marriage and eradicate the "blur" of her life outside of work.

To have it all you must mix and match, chip and shape, give and take with everything that's involved in your all—the interests and the people. Like CEO Jack said, interests get used up, then you change them and go on. The same is true for your all. Things change. But as long as you stay aware of shifts in the whole picture, you'll stay in control.

While Don Wass was running his training company, to keep the alls together he gave up one love, golf, to spend time with another love, his family. It gave him four more hours two times a week with them that he didn't have before. Plus he spent some of the big bucks he'd earned and bought vacation homes on a lake and at a ski resort so weekends could be spent having fun with the family. On his twenty-fifth wedding anniversary he took all of them to Europe for a month.

When consultant Joyce Scott has client appointments that cut into designated exercise time, she asks the clients if they'll go for a walk with her while they talk and work out a problem. She says, "I don't believe anytime I made money I didn't follow my heart. But I also always inserted the right system, the right objective to make things happen."

Attorney Lawrence Land relegates the physical side of his all to less than prime time, so there is no downtime. Land watches videotapes of famous lawyers while on the treadmill every morning and listens to cassettes in his car.

A female client of mine returned from maternity leave and we were discussing what she would have done differently in dealing with the whole event. "I had put together an exhaustive pre–maternity leave to-do list every day and worked to get it all complete. I didn't want to leave loose ends for my people while I was gone. The mistake I made was I forgot to add 'be a healthy incubator' to the list. That was my *personal* job at the time and I hurt my health because I didn't maintain that balance."

You have to be aware of the mixing and matching of activities necessary to work toward your goals. If you don't, you will have to start—if you want to make $100K. Every day you make a responsible and conscious choice.

At times, it is your choice to do as cartoonist Ashleigh Brilliant writes: "Some of my best living has been done when I really should have been doing something else." That's choice. Money buys choice, by the way.

Clearly know the things that make up your all. WRITE THEM DOWN. Keep them handy and refer to them often—fifteen times a day.

Once you know what makes up your all, every day take at least four minutes for each ingredient. Why four? One or two is too little. Brushing your teeth takes that long. Three just isn't enough. Four minutes often gets turned into five, six, or seven, which is good, as long as there is a reasonable balance.

Let's say the following list makes up some of your all. Here are some four-minute tasks to do with each:

- *Professional development.* Try a new way to tell the boss no. Consider the risk, consider the alternative, try out some options, then do it. At the same time, finish a task she needs you to do before she asks you to do it.

- *Family.* Inquire about your partner's day the minute you see him or her. Sit down and listen attentively, like you would listen to your company president explain something. Do not pet the dog, pick up the paper or the mail, turn on the television, or go for the refrigerator while your partner is talking.
- *A Friend.* Ask how you can help her to meet one of her goals.
- *A Customer.* Check his satisfaction on a product you shipped six months ago.
- *Health.* Have the restaurant waiter remove your plate during the business lunch when you've finished half of it.
- *Appearance.* Smile, nod, and say hello to ten different people as you walk through the airport concourse to your plane.
- *Future.* Write a note to the man featured on the front center column of the *Wall Street Journal* about your support of his work. Insert your business card.
- *Church.* Stuff a hundred envelopes for the spring fund-raiser.
- *Clubs.* Volunteer to pick up the keynote speaker for the monthly meeting at the airport next week.

If you spent four minutes for every item on a list like this, it would only add up to thirty-six minutes of your day! Surely you can find that much time, particularly when some of it can be done on the car phone while stuck in traffic anyway. If you don't work on balance, all day, every day—the days, months, and years will fly by while you are standing there out of control.

Keeping a solid foundation makes for happiness like in one Calvin & Hobbes cartoon: The two are standing together, looking out the window, and Calvin says, "In the *short* term, it would make me happy to go play outside. . . . In the long term, it would make me happier to do well at school and become successful." And, as they are careening down a hill together on a snowsled, "But in the *very* long term, I know which will make better memories." Balance your alls.

Add four minutes for anyone and anything else important to your life. And, of course, meanwhile do an exemplary job at your profession.

Work at work that interests you—at least a little—initially. You may find, as you get better at whatever you're doing, you will like it more. You may discover a real passion for it. You may add to your alls in ways you hadn't anticipated.

Or you may learn your chosen route is the pits. If that is the case, salvage what you can from the experience and quickly move to a more fitting situation. Realize no spot is perfect for anyone 100 percent of the time—not for the president of your company or the president of the United States. Your passion always evolves.

Jobs have lives, like companies and people do. Accept the fact that there will be a time when you are in the winter of your job's existence either because of personal interest or the economy. Take on something different that fits your evolving alls. (You know what they are if you are constantly chipping and shaping, giving and taking—writing down and rewriting—everything involved in your all.)

If your work interests you, you'll likely be good at it. If you're good at it, you'll have a chance of making big money. For the amount of effort you will have to put in, the level of intensity necessary, you'd better find it interesting. If you hate it, there isn't enough money out there to keep you doing it really well for the length of time required.

Engaging in work you love is like a high. The catch is, what you love must be of value to others. People aren't financially successful, even if they love what they do, if no one buys what they do.

Work with Intensity

People like to say, "Work smarter, not harder." That's incorrect. You have to toil smarter *and* harder. A lot of things don't work no matter how cleverly executed, unless lots of effort is behind them.

Even if your chosen work turns out to be wrong for you, if you do it with tremendous intensity, you'll develop good habits. And other opportunities will pop up that you hadn't expected. Pick and choose and shape what you're working on with heart and soul, and you eventually might find you love it. Unfortunately, five or six projects you are working on and like to do may not turn out to be productive or profitable. Plod on with fun, don't worry, don't have too many preconceived plans. Keep trying, choosing, and shaping.

The big advantage of hard work, sacrifice, and the experience of misery that sometimes comes with working intensely is that they contribute so much to the enjoyment of the eventual happiness and achievement.

Ideally, you could work less, make more money, and have more time at home . . . but it doesn't typically work out that way. A marketing executive at Microsoft told me about going to the office on Christmas morning to pick up something he'd left for the family celebration. Since he'd been out of town a few days, he answered some E-mail. One was from Bill Gates. He immediately received a response because Gates was working Christmas morning! When it was announced that Gates's wife was pregnant, the business publications reported that his competitors were ecstatic. They hoped he would lose some of his intensity and focus toward his company as he added something new to his all.

Some $100K Club members say, "I always thought the further up the organization you go, the easier it got." Wrong. It gets more intense. You aren't doing the same things as before, but it's not any easier. One example is how you deal with frustration and rejection. It takes intensity to not let it defeat you. You have to refuse to give up. Success in life often comes from simply getting up one more time than you fall.

One $100K Club member, a CFO, said, "The biggest revelation in my career was that not everyone was as intense and driven as I was. But I also learned, you don't want everyone to be that way . . . not your subordinates and not your competitors."

To work with intensity, you must plan targets, steps, and measurements. You have to think each out, clear through a deadline. Each step has to have a timetable or level. Meeting the deadline becomes a measurement.

When you work at something, do it intensely, even as you change what you're working on. When you think about a goal, say to yourself, "I want this ____ to happen, or something *better.*"

Accept the fact that no matter how thought-out your plans, surprises will happen. So plan for them. For example, if you miss a two-month deadline, have in mind steps you can take to compensate. You have to be flexible with movement in the necessary direction. Plan for a surprise that could happen when a windfall occurs that takes you several steps *forward* too.

Humans are good at setting and reaching goals in everyday life. Aspiring $100K Club members just have to be better at it and do more of it. Think about it: Almost everything that happens in your life is due to a form of target-setting.

You want to see the new Bruce Willis movie. The next free evening, when your girlfriend wants to go out, you take her to the movie. You have reached a target.

You want a new fleece shirt jacket. The after-Christmas ads shout 50 percent off. You buy a forest-green, zipper-fronted jacket just like you had in mind.

Lasagna sounds good for supper. You take a frozen lasagna dinner from the freezer and bake it or go to that new Italian place on the corner.

You want to go to Hawaii. You check it out with your husband. He wants to also. You call the airline to check the number of free miles you've racked up. You discover you have enough for two free tickets. You pull out your calendar. You set a tentative date. Confirm it with the boss. Pick up the tickets. Pack your clothes.

Every little and big thing that occurs in your life is the result of some small or large target. You set a goal. True, some occurrences come as surprises; to handle the unexpected, you simply aim in another direction.

Apply that same deliberateness toward earning $100K.

Right now, admit that $100K is a real target (*or something better*). So what might you do today—this minute, this morning—to get closer to that target? (Recommendation: Go to your list of alls and give each one at least four minutes today.)

One morning in 1985 comedian Jim Carrey took a step toward his target: He wrote himself a check for $10 million for acting services. He kept the check, along with a handwritten note that read, "I'll earn this by the year 1995" in his wallet. It happened. He simply says, "It's surreal." It sure is!

Six-time All-Around Champion Cowboy Ty Murray says he wanted to be All-Around Cowboy Champion since he was two years old. He probably picked up the stick horse from the floor right then and there and rode it around a few hours.

Be—almost—unrealistic in your goal setting. Realistic is usually way too limiting.

Eddie George was eight years old when he told his mother he was going to win the Heisman Trophy. In 1995, the Ohio State tailback kept his word. He didn't make it happen from sitting and watching television, but from taking action.

Some simple truths about good, old-fashioned target-setting:

- Goals have to be fierce ones (for big success).
- The dream is in your head, but realization is in your hands.
- Energy added to your desire creates your wish.

What enables success in target-setting is, one, measuring, and two, being willing to give up things that won't produce productive steps that will lead toward your purpose.

And remember this: If you don't expect much, you won't get much.

Maintain a Level of Fun at All Times, Even When It Isn't

If your target is to make big money, that alone will generally be fun as you achieve it. If you are doing something you don't like, despite the moneymaking potential, it won't be fun.

Fun might mean just keeping things challenging. If it isn't challenging, it isn't fun. There are gradations of happiness just as there are gradations of money, and you should always be ready to take the next step.

Fun might just mean doing whatever you're doing right—the first time. Then you'll have time for the really fun stuff.

Take what you do seriously, but don't take yourself so seriously. I know that is advice you have heard before, but have you consistently taken it to heart? I can assure you, if you do something every day toward your alls (even if it is just four minutes' worth), you'll be happier and measurably more successful then the majority of the population.

An interesting fact: Only 24 percent of state lottery winners stopped working after hitting a jackpot, the rest either loved their work or loved *to* work. If you love what you're doing, you never know when the day begins or ends. It's more fun than it is work.

If you maintain a level of fun, you won't develop an aura of desperation. Because if people around you sense desperation, they will avoid you. Plus they may likely withhold support and confidence in you.

You cannot enjoy yourself only occasionally or periodically. You must do it persistently and consistently. No shortcuts here.

Truth is, there is more fun to be had in the higher-up jobs than in entry-level ones. You get to be the decision maker instead of being told what to do. That's fun. You have control and influence. That's fun. It's better than being a pawn moved on a chessboard.

But if you're not yet where you want to be, carry on with a reasonable attitude of fun. Most of your labor will not be especially joyful unless you make it so.

It sounds laughable, but I've seen it happen and therefore caution you against it: Don't become so rich you have no time to laugh.

Have Faith in Yourself So You'll Take Necessary Plunges

The only way to make sure you never fall down is to never try. That's not having fun, nor working intensely on quality of life. When you courageously double your effort, you stay in the game. About 70 percent of people in society are risk-aversive. That means only 30 percent are happily and seriously striving for a better quality in their lives.

A headhunter friend attributes his happy, balanced life

to an upbringing that stressed maintaining good attitudes. Despite some relatively negative experiences—at sixteen his parents divorced and subsequently each remarried twice, his sister has had a lifelong illness—he remains positive. His wife is equally positive despite a negative upbringing. Their joint attitudes enable them to take risks as a team to work toward their predetermined and agreed-upon family alls.

You'll overcome fears when you are making decisions based on your balanced ambitions. Rethink your choices and take different directions. That's just shaping your all. That's a good thing. We all occasionally question the road we've chosen—and question ourselves.

Madonna told of a dream she had one night where she opened up *Billboard* magazine and her song had dropped to number three. Whitney Houston was in the number one spot. Then she went down the hall to her voice coach and the coach was humming Houston's song. We all have those self-questioning moments. The ones who go on to make the big money don't let their thoughts submarine them.

Have confidence you will do well, so that you don't worry about it. Worry makes you vulnerable, and you cling to anything out of desperation. Once you cling to something, you are bound to get exhausted or exhaust whomever or whatever you are clinging to. The result is that someone else controls you. That does not make for happiness.

If you don't have confidence in yourself, then even

when you're financially successful, you'll wonder if you're worthy of it.

Have faith in yourself—that's the only security you've got. You're worth the effort.

Get Along with People

It's critical to get along with people for long-term personal and professional success of any kind.

Social characteristics—good interpersonal and communication skills—are important in making big money. As you move up an organization, you will have more friends. Why is that important? You'll have fewer enemies, and therefore fewer people to torpedo you.

I'll frequently ask $100K Club members what is the toughest thing they deal with. It isn't selling, getting deals done, or putting organizations together. They tell me the difficulty lies in getting along with people. (My first book, *Lions Don't Need to Roar,* deals in-depth with the people-skills side of business. Read it as a guide to stand out, yet fill in, with people around you.)

As the Peanuts cartoon character Linus asks: "If you work real hard, and you get everything you've always wanted, is it worth it?" Snoopy answers, "Not if your dog doesn't like you."

My friend Larry is dating a woman he is truly fond of. As a retired CEO and longtime big moneymaker, he knows the value of getting along with people. Last time we talked, he happily reported, "I've gotten her grandkids to like me!"

"How did you make that happen?" I asked.

"Well, the three-year-old wanted to play 'king,' so I went down to the basement with him, put a blanket he wanted me to wear [like a cloak] around my shoulders, and sat there for two hours playing king."

Like every aspect of following your heart to earn six figures, getting along with people requires choice, decision, and some sacrifice. One part of this skill is deliberately selecting the people you want to be around. Don't continue relationships that are destructive to any part of your all. Similarly, don't foster any behavior that keeps you from being the kind of person you want to be en route to becoming a contented $100K Club member.

Very few people are successful on their own. You need to create an environment in which people are comfortable with you, trust you, and feel they are a part of what's going on—if you are to be successful. Leadership is consensual; people allow you to lead. They'll follow you if they get along with you.

Getting along with people helps you, one, become a $100K Club member, two, handle the inevitable setbacks, and three, enjoy the success a whole lot more.

One CEO I know with a penchant for learning about others frequently asks people at cocktail parties, "If you could do anything, regardless of education or training, what would it be?" He says 99 percent of the time people want to do something other than what they are doing. They say something like, "I really want to . . ."

Then he asks them, "What's stopping you?" And they start giving excuses. He says, "The smart ones soon see the folly of their excuses."

The CEO told me, "The worst thing in the world to me is the thought of being eighty-five years old, sitting in a rocking chair on a porch in Florida and asking myself, 'Why didn't I take more risks? What held me back? What stopped me?' Much better to say, 'I lived and failed at things, but at least I gave it a shot!' "

There is nobody I admire more than people who *do what they want* and make money doing it.

Look at yourself as if you were a corporation. You need a balanced set of skills for success. Find your alls so you can see what's going to make you valuable—what you need to add to and take away. You might get achievement without balance, but you will be one-dimensional, unhappy a lot of the time, and not able to sustain financial success.

A SIX-FIGURE INCOME WILL BE EASY FOR YOU, IF YOU REMEMBER . . .

Balance is relative. It depends on philosophy of life, how you look at things, and how you treat people.

Balance that gives you happiness is like an investment portfolio. Sometimes it's up, sometimes it's down. You just need to be on the plus side *overall.*

When you are true to your heart, you reap many benefits:

You keep your family intact. Being surrounded by loved ones is comforting and pleasant during the ups and downs of a career.

You stay sharp. Remaining on a learning curve all of your life will literally add years to your life. (One approach, according to a recent study: The way to add to your life is to marry a person smarter than you are.)

You stay flexible because you are able to adapt to new situations. You keep your patience. Worry and stress about financial success happening instantly is a waste of time and energy. Have faith it will happen.

You set goals. And they get met.

And—very important, as it relates to this book—*you keep on top of the socioeconomic heap.* With a high income, a challenging and interesting job, you (admit it) get more toys.

The bottom line to remember: If earning six figures were easy, everybody would be doing it. BUT, if you do it right, it *is* easy!

"Figure out what big money means to you—power, respect from parents, lovers, peers, yourself, freedom from poverty, freedom to travel, whatever. Focus on what you want to accomplish besides money and find out what you want to do to make the money. What are you willing to trade off, now and later? When you understand the reason for your particular goal and when in life you want to reach it, go for it. And don't put a cap on what you want to make."

—STEVE BINDER,
Everen Securities

"Try to find a business that really turns you on—even if the job immediately available doesn't necessarily do so. That way you can operate on two levels, doing your job creatively and well while subtly thinking, planning, and probing for a role in the company that truly excites you."

—MIKE COHN,
President, Cohn Literary Agency

"Earning power increases over the course of a career with a person's growth in the Three Ss: Skills, Street Smarts, *and* Social Savvy.

"In the 'new economy,' there is a premium placed on flexibility, breadth, project-based work, and the ability to learn quickly and get results. The old functional silos of finance, marketing, and manufacturing are dead."

—CRAIG WATSON,
Chief Financial Officer,
FMC Asia-Pacific

CHAPTER 3

Opportunities: What Jobs Pay $100K

When you think about making $100K, your first image is often a corporate-type job. Become a senior manager and you'll be on your way. That was more true in the old days. Now there are more creative, unusual, and fun ways to join the $100K Club than ever before.

I'll begin this chapter with several examples of people making interesting money doing work outside of a corporate career. It will put unusual occupations and their subsequent pay into perspective.

But I have also included at the end of this chapter the latest census statistics on jobs in the corporate mainstream: starting pay, average pay, and top pay. If you are choosing the mainstream business route, you will want to review the stats of the job function you're in to make sure it's an area where top pay can at least break the six-figure mark.

If the job track you're working in does not pass the

mark statistically, no matter how well you perform, it will be extra difficult to reach your monetary goals. It is never impossible (remember the police officer, schoolteacher, and military men from the previous chapter). It just might mean that you have to plan to move into other job functions, using your current route as a springboard.

Whether your all leads to typical or atypical work, more *enter* every field than *excel.* It takes different skills to excel in a corporate environment than in a self-employed entrepreneurial manner—both of which will be discussed in Chapters 5 and 6.

For success in any walk of business life there are basic requirements. Every successful person has specific traits that will be discussed in this chapter: the traits that make the difference between the "stars" and the "also-rans."

But first let's look at a variety of unusual ways people are making big money.

Of course, professional athletes make the bucks. We've all read about the multimillion-dollar contracts of the Wayne Gretzkys, Michael Jordans, John Elways, and Picabo Streets of the world. You don't have to be an athletic superstar to make six figures. The lowest-paid rookie on the Denver Broncos football team makes $118K.

Bullrider Tuff Hedeman stays on a bull for eight seconds approximately thirty-two times a year and he makes over $100K. Etbauer brothers Robert, Dan, and Billy have stayed on saddle broncs for those eight seconds (several times a year) and they too earned over

$100K each. At the 1994 National Finals Rodeo, Billy Etbauer won $100K in ten days alone!

The owner of Grindstone, the Kentucky Derby winner, earned $884K for the race. The owner of the second-place winner got $170K.

The 1996 Hawaiian Open purse went to Jim Furyk—$216K. "Winning the money was great, but saying I won the Hawaiian Open title is the best," he said.

Even surfer dudes can make the big bucks—World Champion title holder Sunny Garcia takes home $500K in prize money and product endorsements to his family each year.

A little less exciting, but equally profitable, is the accountant in California, who bought the "right" house, waited eight months, sold it, and moved to Wyoming. By being in an area that experienced huge inflation, he got a $100K windfall in one day (or eight months, depending on how you look at it).

Federal Express pilots make $150K a year flying packages.

A *Playboy* playmate of the year gets $100K plus a car.

The president of the United States earns $200K plus a $50K entertainment allowance.

There is a writer in Texas whose specialty is developing the concept and writing the copy for the lottery scratch games that are so popular nationwide. He dreams up themes, designs layout, clears details with lawyers, develops advertising slogans, supervises the highly specialized printing process, answers calls about players' fulfillment . . . and collects over $200K for his creativity.

A member of the New York Philharmonic can earn $130K.

Numerous long-distance truck drivers living in the Northwest make over $100K a year.

A Shell employee (now former employee) saw the need to have a current database of the nearly five thousand Shell stations, jobbers, and dealers selling Shell products around the country. As big a company as Shell is, no one ever kept track of the names, addresses, and other numbers of their independent reps, which changed daily. The Shell employee, a secretary, took it upon herself to update the list. Updated material, done on her own time, became *her* property. She quit her job and sold the information back to Shell. They were very happy because it was the first time they ever had current, accurate data. Her database business brings her well over $150K annually—far more than the secretarial job!

Retired Chrysler Chairman Lee Iacocca gets $500K a year for consulting to Chrysler.

A man who flies the oil pipelines around the world, checking for cracks, makes six figures.

A woman in the Midwest scouts the world for unused (new but old) parts for Model A automobiles, bringing in well over $100K a year.

An entrepreneurial father and son in Nevada play golf during the week. Then on weekends they drive a customized refrigerated truck twelve hours back and forth every Friday and Saturday between flower growers in Carpinteria, California, and florists in Las Vegas. Weekly sales are $10,000, which is well over $500K a year between the two.

A twenty-seven-year-old female Realtor in an Oregon town with a population of one thousand listed and sold within a month a $3 million ranch. Her commission: $210K.

And there's the Hollywood version of at least six figures: Courtney Cox, who plays the character Monica Geller on the television show *Friends,* makes $500K a season. Kelsey Grammer, who stars on *Frasier,* gets $150K per episode (ten episodes per season). The people who do the silk flower arrangements for the backdrop of these television shows have $100K-plus salaries! Brooke Shields *turned down* $350K for a NordicTrack fitness machine advertisement. Of course, rock star and actress Courtney Love makes well into seven figures for her talent. (So she can afford to pay $100K a year to the individual who provides security and maintenance at the cemetery where the ashes of her late husband, Kurt Cobain, are buried.)

Skycaps at Los Angeles International Airport are rumored to make $100K in tips. (It's an unwritten rule that they don't discuss it, for obvious reasons.) Other "tip" earners at the six-figure financial level include some table dancers in topless bars.

A trust-fund baby in Boulder, Colorado, can't touch his million-dollar inheritance but can use the interest he earns on it. A 10 percent return on his investment gives him $100K a year.

Bay Buchanan ran her brother Pat's unsuccessful presidential campaign bid and took home $100K.

A millionaire in Vancouver, British Columbia, sells marijuana seeds to Americans who turn around and make

$100K a year by growing and distributing plants. An article about him on the front page of the *Wall Street Journal,* complete with picture, explains his public persona: The police look the other way because of his up-front business style and the fact that he pays Canadian taxes on the illegal business (some $250K in U.S. dollars a year).

A former butcher who foresaw bison as the "meat of the future" now sells twenty thousand pounds of meat to Japan every month, putting him into the $100K Club.

A man, wife, son, and daughter make up a team that earn well into six figures "facilitating" deals. They put "people with money" together with "people who need money"—typically groups of people who would never find each other otherwise, such as sponsors for race car owners, products for home shopping networks, farmers with raw materials for manufacturers needing to fill plant production time, large-volume truckloads of product (like cotton bath towels made in Poland) to retailers like Wal-Mart. Their motto is, "You never know where the money is."

A gun salesman fiddles around in his basement customizing gun stocks for special customers. Four years later he has a niche specializing in commemorative rifles that is so successful, Winchester tries to buy him out for $4 million.

Native American Indian Ray Tracy crafts custom jewelry. From humble Navajo reservation beginnings he now has showrooms in Santa Fe and Atlanta.

Chess champion Gary Kasparov worked eight days in a row playing chess against IBM's Deep Blue computer in 1995 and got $400K for his victory. "At the end,

I was a lot more tired and stressed than the computer was," Kasparov admitted.

That's just a *short* list of real people (like you and me!)—well, except for the chess champion, bullrider, surfer, movie star, table dancer, and drug dealer—making big money by utilizing their all.

In a way, they developed survival skills for the twenty-first century by adopting nontraditional methods to make big money. Whatever direction interests you: The most important thing to remember is, more enter than excel.

More Enter than Excel in *Anything*

The ones who are motivated to excel, as opposed to those who just enter a field and look for their comfort zone, have set themselves apart. It isn't IQ that is the difference, but rather what they are willing to do.

Although a lot of the examples I've just given could suggest that mostly the young make $100K in unusual ways, that is not the case.

Age, as it relates to money, was expressed wonderfully by an unknown author who wrote, "Age is not a time in your life as much as a state of mind. The ability to succeed depends on your will, quality of imagination, vigor in emotion, courage over timidity, appetite for adventure over ease. You're as young as your faith and as old as your doubt, as young as your self-confidence, as old as your fear, young as your hope, old as your despair. If your heart accepts messages of beauty, cheer, courage, grandeur, and power from nature, you will be young forever."

People who excel possess certain traits—regardless of their age. This chapter reports on those traits. Presented here are the "thought" and "work" patterns that manifest money.

So what makes the difference regardless of age, race, sex? First, these people *want* to join the rarefied status of $100K Club members. They decide it is important to them. Second, they take responsibility for judgments they make along the way. They prioritize and keep prioritizing over time. And third, they attempt to:

- Be a person of substance
- *Try*
- Lose early, lose (kinda) big, and lose often
- Be tenacious
- Study all the time
- Learn to *live with it*
- Do more than necessary, then keep doing it
- Never assume
- Eliminate excuses and needless work

Be a Person of Substance

You *have* to build a successful track record in whatever you do. There is just no way around this one.

Decide where money comes from in your field. Typically it comes from customers. Find out who the customers are, find out what they want. If you can't find that out, how can you be a person of substance and deliver?

If you can't build a case for your direct contributions toward profits, why should anyone pay you anything? For the last three years of your endeavors you need to be able to attach real numbers to your worth. Your worth to the organization is roughly described as: profit from revenues added to customer satisfaction.

Often it doesn't matter how hard you work. What matters is the results you produce.

An IBMer and $100K Club member I know just turned down a job offer with another company that would have paid him four times his age and twice what he's currently making. Why? He's happy where he is. He's not stupid, though. He knows how to build a case for himself if IBM should become unhappy with him. He can document how his salary is paid back many times over through profits from revenues he generates.

It's unlikely that the company will become unhappy with him, however. An objective third party was hired to interview the IBMer's biggest customer and rate him in six areas: partnership development, responsiveness to problems, support in problem solving, quality of service, value added to the customer, and skills in general. How was the IBMer rated? A hundred percent in every category! His boss's annual performance appraisal also rated him "extraordinary." That's a person of substance. That's a $100K Club member.

It's very important to keep in mind while you are working that you do it for results. An awful lot of people in corporate America put in "clock" hours but not "productive to the bottom line" hours. Notice that I wrote earlier that it doesn't matter how hard you work or how long: It's how *well.* And you know in your heart when you're doing well or not.

I remember when I first started my business over twenty years ago. I hadn't learned about quality of work over quantity of work. I'd call my parents to say I had to work on a weekend instead of visit. My dad would kiddingly challenge me with, "Business, or monkey business?" I'd protest, "Business, of course." Then I had to stick to my word and make sure it was good business work that produced some real results. (It's easy for lots of people to do "monkey business" between eight and five, Monday through Friday, as well.)

Try

When things don't look bright, sometimes to *try* is all that will get you through. You don't quit: you just go on. Turn everything around to positive instead of laboring in the negative. Keep your calm. Even when not feeling 100 percent, put out the effort. The one who puts out the biggest effort almost always wins. In the rodeo world they call this "cowboy up." The Finnish have a word for it: *sisu,* which means having the courage to never give up.

In Hollywood there are fifty thousand people in the Screen Actors Guild. Less than 2 percent make over $10K a year. A lot more enter than excel in the field. Who succeeds in Hollywood? As in most places, it's those who stay persistent, perfect their craft, make contacts, do side jobs as necessary, understand the business side as well as the talent side of their work, pursue both, and try. Some people stay in acting class forever, though. They study, but they never work. The same is true of certain people in all other professions: they procrastinate until they coagulate. They go through the motions but don't provide substance.

In all work there is frustration. Sometimes people with very little talent do well and those with incredible talent aren't working. But in general, the better you are, the more you work—whether you're in Hollywood or Cleveland.

An actor friend of mine, Walter Olkewicz, had a recent part on the television comedy *Seinfeld.* He told me, "That show is good because everyone works so hard on it. The man who plays Kramer (Michael Richards), for example, works every minute in making the show better. Off camera, he keeps going over lines in his head; he tries this look versus that look." That's *try.*

A winning college basketball coach said, "We try to play to win instead of play not to lose." (Think about it; it's an entirely different attitude if you're earning your money for a better quality of life rather than just to get by.) The coach's players' *try* is to refuse to lose. They've lived that attitude the last five winning seasons.

I'd rather be one who has tried and failed than one who has failed to try.

Lose Early, Lose (Kinda) Big, and Lose Often

But *not* in the same type of situation. In other words, don't repeat the same mistakes. That would mean you aren't learning. The goal here is to gain from errors.

The annual report of Western Pacific Airlines lists the tenure of their company president, Edward Beauvais, as a *risk factor.* Pretty unusual admission. Beauvais admits he made mistakes and insists "the lessons will be heeded" from his experience running America West Airlines into filing Chapter Eleven.

Joe Markham took twenty-three years to get his dog-toy invention turned into a $5 million business. He survived near poverty, lawsuits, and bankruptcy during those years. But today he says, "I look back now and say, 'Thank you, Lord, for my trials,' because they made me tenacious."

Dallas Cowboys quarterback Troy Aikman admits he hates to lose. Always has, even as a boy. But he also readily admits that's where he learned and built character and skill.

"No one cares if everything is right all of the time. We'd be in the banking business if we wanted to be one hundred percent. Sure, mistakes cost money, but they aren't life-threatening," says John Ameran, CEO of Mattel, Inc.

You've heard the cliché, "The greatest mistake is the fear of making one." True words. I've seen far too many people in my professional life who are so afraid of messing up that they are a pathetic mess.

If you see someone lose, don't say, "Oh, that poor person." Instead, look at the winner and say, "Oh, that poor person." The one who loses acquires knowledge. The one who wins, just wins. Ask yourself, when everything went well in a situation, what did you master or learn? Probably little, except the fact that it feels good to win. But when you've failed, you might have picked apart your performance, sought outside help, tried a new skill, worked harder, and generally made yourself better for the next time.

I'm a pretty fortunate individual, both personally and professionally. And I'm grateful for that and appreciative. I also recognize that when things are going so well, I can get "soft" in my skills. Occasionally I'll say to my secretary, "We *need* a problem around here.

Things are going too well. I could use a setback to overcome." She laughs, but she knows what I mean.

Sometimes I'll take an hour and mentally hypothesize about a current project and "worst case" it. I'll think about and even write down the bad turn of events that could happen. Then I come up with solutions. I learn from my analysis of this problem *that does not yet exist.* If something should explode, I've already rehearsed some solutions. If nothing does, the mental exercise keeps me sharp for the thing that I didn't anticipate and helps me minimize facing the three W's in business: What went wrong!

From setbacks, you also learn that losing is not pleasant, that you dislike it, that you're determined to change, and that you enjoy the feeling of winning even more after having lost. Don't be afraid to lose; nothing builds character like a setback handled well.

How? Reflect on the situation, evaluate it, and decide what you'll do. Then do it. And don't worry, as they say in rodeo: The ground will always catch you.

Sometimes a "loss" is a simple misunderstanding in which someone misinterpreted your intent. That is good to experience also. If it was all or almost all your fault and you really must apologize, do it as soon as possible. Whether on the telephone, face-to-face, or in a letter, use these words: "I apologize from the bottom of my heart."

Why bother with the drama? Because it shows your seriousness and sincerity. People notice, appreciate, and tend to believe you. Think about it: How would you react to a friend saying to you "I'm sorry" versus "I apologize from the bottom of my heart"? (Yes, it's okay for a man to say this—it's not for women only.)

The admonition to lose early, (kinda) big, and often is meant as encouragement to take risks early on in life. The most difficult client I have is an individual who has sailed through life up until about age thirty with no problems and all of a sudden is hit with a major or even minor obstacle and is totally unprepared to handle it—because he or she hasn't learned from defeats along the way. From pain, you learn, period.

"Lose (kinda) big" means make sure you are trying hard enough, stretching seriously enough to cause some difference, whether you succeed or fail. Losing (kinda) big does not mean accidentally placing the postage stamp upside down on a letter to a customer. Losing real big—which I am *not* promoting—falls into only three categories: lying, cheating, or stealing to succeed. You will truly be a genuine loser of that is how you work toward your goals.

You should make it a practice to reflect on your day, probably just before you go to sleep, and ask yourself, "Where did I mess up today and what did I learn from it?" Answer. Get up and write it down if necessary. Then ask, "What did I do supremely well today and what did I learn from it?" Answer. Daily you should be able to specifically point to lessons acquired from both situations.

That's where "lose often" comes in. View it as a badge of courage, not as a sign of defeat, to stretch, slip up, recover . . . stretch, slip up, recover, leap forward . . . and just keep doing it, far past your peers.

Also, consider the fact that there probably has to be a finite number of mistakes a human being can make in a lifetime, as long as they don't recur. So get through them early on!

Every step is not forward; lots are backward. Keep persevering. Instead of obsessing about today's setback, consider that a career is made up of approximately 12,500 days. You can afford a few bad ones.

If you don't know how to lose, you don't know how to live.

Be Tenacious

We all know stick-to-itiveness is necessary for success in anything. Tenacity isn't taking a stab at something two or even three times. It's doing it twenty-six times if necessary.

A very tenacious $100K Club member told me about trying to set up a meeting with someone. "I needed an appointment with him, so I called and left a message on his voice mail. Two days later I left another message. Every two days after that, for one week, I left a message along with my 800 number. Then the next Monday I called and left a message at six, eight, ten A.M., twelve, two, and four P.M. The next day I did the same thing—six, eight, ten, twelve, two, and four o'clock. The next day, after my six A.M. phone message, I got a call back from him. He said (with a chuckle in his voice) he was getting tired of hearing my 800 number. He asked what I wanted, and I told him. He agreed to a meeting."

I asked him, "Don't you risk becoming irritating to the person?"

He answered, "I've found that good businesspeople will tell you if you are a pain. And when they do, you can ask, 'What do you want me to do to get your business?' I also tell them if I can't achieve what they need, I'll leave them alone—but first I have to have the opportunity to show them." He went on to say, "If they lack the confidence to say outright 'Leave me alone,' they deserve to be hassled. If no one ever irritated someone, nothing would ever get done. If the person is so insecure as to not give me the time to explain what I have to offer, I go above them. I write a nice letter to the boss saying I was not happy with the response to my proposal from his subordinate and feel I have a product worth viewing. I'm willing to go to the top and grit my teeth for the possible downside of my action."

When he told me this story, I tried to put myself in the buyer's place. I too would have called someone who phoned me that often, more out of curiosity than irritation. I can also recall times I hated to say no to someone and just avoided calling back. That specific $100K Club member doesn't let people treat him that way. That might be one of the reasons he makes the big money.

There were many messages we received as children that are counterproductive to aggressively going after targets:

- Don't be pushy.
- Don't take chances.
- Take your turn.
- Speak only when spoken to.

As adults trying to fulfill our all, we have to take authority, take risks, take accountability, yet be affable at the same time. That can run counter to early indoctrination.

In the dictionary the word *power* has a primary definition of "simple effectiveness." To be simply effective, state what you want, predict (or anticipate) the result, alter your approach to fit the situation, and take the risks. I always advise people to practice on small things, where the result isn't critical.

The man who made the persistent phone calls followed that prescribed sequence. He knew what he wanted: an appointment. He anticipated reticence on the buyer's part but left the necessary message. He didn't get a response, so he altered his approach to bombard the client with messages. It was risky. Fortunately, it turned out well. Who knows what would have happened if he had politely left the typical three attempts and gone on in discouragement.

Mike Holmgren, coach of the Green Bay Packers, explained his team's attempt to stop San Francisco's running game when the Packers weren't known for that strength: "If you don't try, they won't have any respect for you whatsoever."

To make the big bucks, you'll run into lots of objections from numerous sources. Roughly 80 percent of people quit an undertaking after one roadblock. Anticipate roadblocks with a positive outlook and accept them as a challenge.

Take, for instance, the objection we all fear: "No." When you get a no, clarify which part of no they mean. It's like the singer Lori Morgan and the words to her song: "What part of no don't you understand?" Does the no mean in this lifetime, this week, today, for the whole department, or what? In other words, get the naysayers to elaborate.

Think back to when you've seen a tenacious child ask his mother for a cookie before supper. "No" is the answer. "Why?" is the child's response. And then "Why?" again. About this time the mother says, "Well, okay, just one." Ninety percent of yeses come after a no. It worked at age eight, and it will work at thirty-eight.

Another way to deal with a no is not to react but to start asking questions. The simplest is to ask, "Oh?" When someone objects to what you want, say, "Oh?" Then shut up. It forces the person to take a stand, explain, defend. When you get the answer, you will understand, and then you can decide what to do about it.

When you ask why you've been told no, ask three times. Use three different ways, of course, so you don't sound tedious. If you ask once, it doesn't make the person think. Two times just tells you a little bit more. Three times and you finally get closer to the truth.

Another way to handle objections is to consider the fact that people can easily think of no more than six objections to any one thing. Think about it. Let's say you don't want to go to your spouse's college buddy's home for the weekend. You can likely come up with no more than six reasons off the top of your head:

- The drive is too long.
- His house is too small for guests.
- His kids are too rowdy.
- He doesn't have cable.
- The weather looks bad.
- The car is acting strangely.

It took several minutes to come up with those objections. True, if I sat down and really concentrated, I could come up with more. But most people don't do that unless they have super-strong motivation.

If you think through the objections and answer them before you get them, you may not get them—or at least you'll be able to handle them when you do.

The wise person would anticipate those objections and handle them in advance: "I want to go to Bob's this weekend. I know it's a long drive, but if we go just twenty miles farther we can visit that inn you read about in the *Hideaway Report.* We can stay there the first night, then the next night we can stay at Bob's. His place is a little small, but the kids are going to be at their grandparents', so it won't seem so bad. They don't have cable yet in their area, but maybe you can think of some videos you'd like to rent and take along. Since the weather is looking bad anyway, we might as well be indoors with friends. If you think this could work, I'll take the car in tomorrow and get that noise taken care of."

Preparing for objection is sort of like inoculating yourself against the flu. You get a shot, you don't get the flu. Same thing with inoculating yourself against objections, obstacles, barriers, and naysayers.

To cover all the bases, think of yourself receiving the proposition you're giving. Think about it from the other side. Write it out as if you were receiving it. Be precise and to the point, so it's easy to read—so your target will want to read it. If you take the few minutes to do this, you will already have won, because you will have learned something.

On an airplane once the person beside me was talking on the telephone. He muttered to me, "This hotshot thinks he knows a lot. I'll let him talk until he's out of breath and then I'll say no." If the "hotshot" had asked the prescribed questions, then inoculated against a no, he might not have received it!

Study All the Time

Everyone and everything. One of the biggest assets of those who excel in a field is their talent to observe.

Most people reading, say, *Forbes* look for the articles of most interest to them. Instead, they could expand their horizons by reading articles on subjects they know the least about, so they can acquire new knowledge.

The late Texan congresswoman Barbara Jordan would say about studying and learning all the time, "I'm going to be the best I can no matter what it takes." Your success will be directly proportional to your willingness to commit to similar excellence.

Studying, as I mean it, is not formal-education booklearning. It's the wisdom that comes from discipline. Discipline of the observant mind, eye, hand, muscle, nerves—the whole body. That's how life is lived in the best way, the happiest, healthiest, and most useful way.

Remember the family whose job is to facilitate putting people with money together with people who need it? You won't find a group of better listeners. Why? They know that when they listen and observe, they learn. One deal that resulted in hundreds of thousands of dollars' income came from a four-hour airplane conversation in which one member of the family sat listening to a businessman's problem. When they hear or learn of a problem, they figure out a way to fix it because that's where their money is.

To study: ask, listen, write down, ask, listen, write down. (Writing down supports your memory, is flattering to the talker, and is sort of a "contract.") When you listen, you learn what your client values and needs so you can determine how to fix the problem.

Studying through listening means to be a true listener. Don't introduce a subject and then tune out the person responding; don't interrupt, cut off, or one-up the other person when you start talking. Have the patience, on the telephone and when meeting face-to-face, to let the other person talk through—without interrupting. Write notes if necessary to remind yourself of what you want to say when the other person finishes.

In this hurry-up world, interruptions occur constantly. You see them at the office, in meetings, at bars. Where groups of people gather and many thoughts are being expressed, it seems like interruptions are acceptable. They aren't. You don't learn in those situations; you only grandstand.

Say you find yourself in such a group. You're listening to someone and another joins you. Don't let the third person interrupt the person talking. You can't always control these situations, but others notice that at least you're making an effort. It makes you stand out. Take, for example, the office Christmas party, and you are talking to the wife of the sales manager. The president of the company comes up. Continue listening to the wife; don't switch to the president because he is "more important." If he dominantly inserts himself, touch the woman on the elbow and say, "I want to continue with your point on __________." Listen to the president. Then when you have a chance, deliberately go back to the wife's topic.

There is a time to talk, and a time to get others to talk while you listen and watch what's going on. If you look for the right give-and-take in a conversation, you'll pick up what the others have in mind and they'll feel that they've been heard.

Asking questions is not a passive activity. Asking

questions is a form of carrying the subject forward and learning about it.

People are either growing up in their business and in their observing, or they are growing old.

Members of the $100K Club are studious observers.

Learn to Live with It

In your personal and professional life there will be people you dislike, even detest. It may be a boss, a boss's boss, co-worker, or customer. It's the person who drives you crazy with the dumb things he or she does. It's the person you always complain about to your spouse or locker-room buddies. You aren't going to change the people you dislike. Learn to live with it.

Learning to live with it doesn't mean taking a passive role. Quite the opposite. You can:

- Ask for what you want, in clear terms.
- Accept the unacceptable response or answer, for now.
- Turn up the work effort—despite the unending frustration.

Few people follow those three simple steps. Most don't clearly state what they want in a nonemotionally charged tone. They argue with, complain about, or flat-out reject the response. Then, to make matters worse, they turn *down* their work effort. That sequence of actions does not help you excel.

A classic example is when an individual gets passed over for a promotion she thought she deserved. The emotionally charged person races into the boss's office to demand why. The boss, now on the defensive, attempts to explain. The individual dismisses the rationale, complains, whines, even threatens to quit. Leaves. And boycotts her work until she calms down. She does the exact opposite of what those who excel do.

Accept irritation as a fact of life, and learn to live with it. Surprisingly, just adopting that attitude shift makes the person or the situation less irritating. As one CEO said to me, humorously referring to his hairline, "I have to accept the fact that I will always have an eight-inch part and learn to live with it."

Or as Shakespeare wrote, "There is nothing either good or bad but thinking makes it so."

Set aside personal differences to accomplish what you want. You'll get respect because you can set personality aside. Remember, you probably only have to deal temporarily with that person or situation. People who treat you poorly have likely had someone else play foul with them long before they met you. They just carry their hidden agenda over when dealing with you. Don't give them that power.

Learning to live with it allows you to be uncomplicated. Uncomplicated people have more energy and time to make the big bucks.

Another thing to learn to live with is the *intensity* required to make six figures. Even when you feel intense, make it look easy. You'll discourage your competition, inspire people above you, and make yourself feel better. Your facial expression, for example, should maintain a relaxed, confident, comfortable, and competent expression—the expression that comes from having a slight smile. (In fact, there is an old Chinese adage: Smiling brings in the money.) Let others see only the intensity you want them to see through your expression and comportment.

Do More than Necessary, Then Keep Doing It

Ask yourself, "What else can I do better or more productive?" Then go do that. If it's worth doing, it's worth doing more of it.

Mark Schneider, son of the president of United International, reveals his dad's secret to success: "My father taught me that you should get out ahead of the next guy and lay a path where others will follow."

It's best if your ideas and work are original. If they aren't original, come up with more of them. Get with the program.

While traveling recently in Hawaii, I bought fresh fruit at roadside stands. One stretch of road had four different stands, all about fifty yards apart. Over a period of time I stopped at each one to compare prices and check quality. Each offered pretty much the same variety, except one might charge fifty cents more or less per pound on the same item. But one of the four stands had an interesting tactic. Every time I made my purchase and headed back toward the car, the seller would call out, "Here, take this also." And he would hand me a free pineapple, a bag of pickled mangoes, or a papaya. Every time I stopped, the same thing happened. Now, which stand do you think I started buying from exclusively? You're right—the one that did more.

There are so many ways to do more. I'll list some to get your own creativity flowing:

Follow up. Some time after you've finished a task, go back to the people involved and check on their satisfaction. Report to them on some new development they might find interesting. Inform them of some aspect of the warranty they might have overlooked. Wish them happy birthday if that's all you can come up with. The point is to go back and follow up, when others don't.

Deliver what you promise. Whatever you casually or seriously commit to—faxing an article, telephoning a customer at a specific time, answering a letter—*do* whatever it is you said you would.

Have more than one solution or idea. Go in with a notebook full of ideas. How do you get more ideas? By paying attention. When you focus your attention, you are more efficient, effective, and flowing in whatever you're doing. Intuition comes from paying attention to what's going on around you.

When you pay attention, you are mindful of what you do that sabotages you. Take interruptions in your work, for example. If someone walks into your office and gives you some new piece of information that will help you achieve that day's target, it isn't an interruption. But if someone comes in and gives you information that is totally irrelevant and useless, yet you listen, that's an interruption. You have to decide what attention to give—how to limit the unending data that can be presented during a day as thought- and time-robbing interruptions.

Seek opportunities to surge. Surge is a strategy in running events. Competitors seize momentum to test the competition, take inventory of what's going on, look for weaknesses, and psyche out the competition. Stay abreast of new developments, both in and out of your field—you may come across an idea that could surge you ahead of your competitors.

I witnessed a form of surging at a restaurant recently. A customer asked a waiter about controlling the uncomfortable air-conditioning. She finished with, "I know it's not your responsibility . . ." He pleasantly responded, "I'll make it my business. And I'll make sure it gets done."

Do anything good you are doing *ten* minutes more than the rest of the people are willing to.

My mother taught in a country school during the mid-1940s. She said, "My attitude was the kids had to know everything I knew. We just didn't go on to another subject unless they did." That "do more" attitude has former students keeping in touch with her fifty years later.

It's like the Nike slogan: "Just do it." But for $100K Club members, the slogan is: "Just do *more* of it." Any time something comes up at work that nobody wants to do, jump on it. Who knows what you'll learn? One man proudly told me, "I landed responsibility for the parking lot and cafeteria that way." He has no idea how that will benefit him, since he's in data processing, but it's sure to teach him some new skills not normally afforded an MIS person.

My editor for this book, Rick Wolff, practices doing more. While reading *Hemisphere* magazine on a recent United Airlines flight, an article caught my attention. It discussed the validity of companies hiring athletic coaches to train their executives. It was well-written, made valid points, and used good humor. After reading it, I checked to see who wrote it. To my surprise, it was *my* Rick Wolff. Rick has a full-time job at Warner Books, but he understands the value of doing more. On his own time he freelances a few articles. How could he possibly benefit from that extra effort?

- He better understands writers, being one himself.
- He keeps his writing skills current rather than concentrating on his editing skills exclusively.
- He gets his name out in the public to people who might not know of him.
- He can feel pride in the accomplishment.
- He has more credits to add to his résumé.

- He'll get published more readily, having been published in *Hemisphere*.
- He made his employer look good because the byline included the name "Warner Books."
- He added to his job security.
- He could possibly get a speaking engagement from some reader who liked what he said and wanted her employees to hear the message.
- He made himself some extra money.

Those benefits seem pretty good for the effort of doing more, don't they?

Two partners in a custom jewelry business used the basement of one of the partners' parents, complete with Ping-Pong table, as their studio. The parents also had a sofa in the basement. Since the partners chose to work twenty-four hours a day, they'd take naps on the sofa, then get up and go back to work. They started their business in 1985 with a $2,000 investment. In 1995 their sales were $1.2 million. They simply did more than the next who entered the jewelry-crafting business.

Choosing not to do more is bargaining with yourself, rationalizing, and cutting corners. It prevents you from excelling in any field.

Sometimes doing more starts by simply ceasing to procrastinate. To minimize procrastination, create a list of tasks that need to be completed for a specific job, highlighting the steps that are most important and the ones that can be done most quickly (or easily). Start with the steps that are *both* important and quick to do.

The result is the beginning of the end to procrastination. Plus it motivates you to keep going because you've made some progress.

Perhaps this book's most valuable benefit to you will be to increase your ability to make yourself do what you have to do, then do more of it, when it should be done, whether you like it or not.

Never Assume

You know the old expression: It makes an *ass* out of *u* and *me*. I know I'm not the first one to tell you that, but it doesn't seem to stop most of us from continuing to do it!

One of the biggest misassumptions people make is job security. They conclude that if they do a good job in corporate America, they will always have one. Wrong. Twenty years ago I was quoted in the *Rocky Mountain News* saying, "Your job is only as secure as the emotions of your immediate superior." I received a lot of flack for that, but it is true nonetheless.

You should not believe (er, assume) you have the right to expect job security. You can prefer it, of course. But it is much wiser to remind yourself of the reality that your job could be gone tomorrow. A *Business Week* survey showed that 71 percent of the workforce feels their boss has too much power over them. I believe, and have experienced, that power is put back into *your* hands when you don't make automatic assumptions.

Job security is a challenge when it comes to *not* assuming. But daily there are numerous opportunities for you not to fall for a misconception.

It doesn't happen very often that people truly understand what you are saying, doing, or thinking. Don't conclude, without checking, that they understand you or believe you are understanding them. You can't assume.

Always check the communication, but don't accept that there is understanding. Clarify what you heard versus what was said. One misconstrued word can change the entire meaning. Simply ask in a noncondescending way, "Let me make sure what you said is what I thought I heard . . ." Any time there is the slightest doubt, ask, "What did you mean by __________?" In business there are too many fluff words and buzzwords people use all the time that in fact mean different things to different people.

Consider a situation in which you are involved with three other people. That means there are four different thought patterns going at the same time. Knowing that gives you ammunition.

It's like I wrote earlier about anticipating objections. Simply slow down, think things through, and consider all points of view; then you'll avoid taking things (and being taken) for granted.

Eliminate Excuses and Needless Work

These excuses can no longer be used:

- I'm too short.
- My spouse won't let me.
- I'd feel like a jerk around my friends.
- "Years ago I went to a fortune-teller and she said . . ."
- I'm not smart enough.
- I'm too old.
- I'm not that lucky.
- The Dow Jones is the problem.

Eliminate needless work that hinders making six figures:

- Phone calls that get lengthy
- Letters that are needlessly wordy
- Speeches that are too long
- Too many personal calls that get too long
- Reading things that don't improve you
- Spending time in activities that don't contribute to your alls
- Spending time with people who hurt you instead of help you

In these lists, consistency is the key. Repeat (repetitively) the more easily adaptable behaviors. For some reason, it seems to take twenty-one aggressive days of new behavior to make it your own. (A lot of experts in the field of human behavior have come up with that figure over the years. Try it for yourself. Select one thing that will make a noticeable change in you. Do it the new way twenty-one days—three weeks solid—and see if the change doesn't feel natural.) Discipline with anything new develops into habit.

If you don't want to wait twenty-one days, then another way to monitor new behavior is by doing things the new way seventy-five times (yes, that is seventy-five) to "own" it. You probably can't get away with doing it once today and once tomorrow. That will take nearly three months before the trait becomes yours. However you do it, it is better to start soon, and better yet to keep at it.

The good news is that in that short three-week period you can change into a new person. The bad news is that in those same three short weeks you can change back into the less-than-effective person—if you let yourself slip.

I had a client who worked with fervor to become a leader in her company. She had been sent to me for private counseling because, although she was brilliant, she didn't have the confidence of others. She needed to learn how to contribute in meetings, speak up, and take control as necessary. After our discussion, her efforts were so intense in changing how she thought, acted, and interrelated that I got word back from the company they would have paid four times my fee based on the results. Six months of excellence. Then one day she slipped up, retreated into her old ineffective behavior. It shook her boss's confidence in her so much that he demoted her. Lesson: Those who wish to excel *keep at it.*

We can't control specific money-earning activities every day of our lives. We *can* control the behaviors that lead to those money-earning activities.

As I promised in the beginning of this chapter, here is a list of professions in which people are making the big money.* The columns show typical starting pay for each job, average pay in the industry, and what the top money earners can make.

Profession	Initial Pay	Industry Average	Typical Top Pay
ACCOUNTING & FINANCE			
Big Six firm	$30,125	$38,625	$69,750
Small firm	24,750	36,500	63,000
CORPORATE ACCOUNTING			
Associate accountant	25,000	28,400	31,200
Senior auditor	37,200	42,500	48,600
Senior tax accountant	46,900	55,300	62,800
Controller	97,900	147,900	176,000
Treasurer	108,000	160,500	191,100
CFO	165,000	277,200	345,000
ADVERTISING			
Copywriter	30,000	50,000	90,000
Art Director	27,500	47,500	82,500

*Data supplied by *Fortune,* June 26, 1995. And note that there are regional differences in these statistics. Jobs in the Northeast and West Coast, for example, typically pay more than do those in the Midwest and South.

Profession	Initial Pay	Industry Average	Typical Top Pay
Account Executive	28,000	62,500	375,000
Creative Executive	150,000	300,000	500,000
ARCHITECTURE			
Architect	27,000	35,000	43,900
Principal/Partner	35,000	50,000	110,000
CEO	1,131,042	1,524,057	2,043,294
CONSULTING			
Strategic consultant	47,677	120,660	307,667
Human resource consultant	38,633	64,218	139,099
MIS con.	39,120	81,569	130,156
CORPORATE ETHICS			
Ethics administrator	35,000	50,000	70,000
VP for ethics	95,000	140,000	200,000
EDUCATION			
University professor	39,050	49,490	63,450
Elementary teacher	26,693	36,357	50,600
Secondary teacher	26,077	37,764	53,300
ENGINEERING			
Biomedical engineer	37,750	72,500	150,000
Chemical engineer	39,863	73,970	179,700
Civil engineer	30,690	62,000	141,260
Electrical engineer	33,000	65,876	146,000
Mechanical engineer	36,935	65,160	155,734
Industrial engineer	35,244	67,000	215,000

Profession	Initial Pay	Industry Average	Typical Top Pay
FINANCIAL SERVICES			
Financial planner	27,000	50,000	200,000
Portfolio manager	40,000	100,000	150,000
Loan officer—mortgage	27,200	54,600	67,800
Loan officer—commercial	41,500	71,000	86,200
Actuary	25,382	36,914	58,432
Life insurance underwriter	23,500	37,564	52,563
Group insurance underwriter	27,421	38,883	56,400
GOVERNMENT JOBS			
Economist	21,486	46,852	102,338
Budget analyst	21,486	38,885	102,338
Personnel manager	18,956	46,852	102,338
Agency head	–	–	148,400
CIA director	–	–	133,600
Congressperson	–	–	133,600
Cabinet member	–	–	148,400
HEALTH CARE			
Family practice physician			
Private practice	86,300	123,700	169,400
HMO provider	96,700	123,300	170,000
Neurosurgeon	158,500	263,300	450,400
Cardiothoracic surgeon	175,900	312,300	435,650
Plastic surgeon	157,500	181,000	341,200
Registered nurse	34,600	39,800	45,700
Licensed physical therapist	35,500	45,500	53,800

Profession	Initial Pay	Industry Average	Typical Top Pay
HIGH TECHNOLOGY			
Software engineer	33,702	54,470	75,524
Hardware engineer	33,952	54,704	75,360
CD-ROM engineer	35,000	60,000	100,000
HUMAN RESOURCES			
Employee training manager	49,500	59,000	65,700
Benefits manager	63,800	85,200	101,600
VP of human resources	118,100	188,700	235,600
INFORMATION SERVICES			
Programming trainee	9,000	19,500	28,000
LAN/WAN specialist	27,900	41,000	49,983
Database specialist	33,228	45,193	69,000
Systems analyst	35,728	44,026	49,270
Applications programmer	25,992	49,000	55,000
MIS director	57,700	89,000	210,000
IRS AGENT			
Tax auditor	19,500	34,000	38,500
Revenue officer	19,500	34,000	66,606
Revenue agent	19,500	49,663	81,013
LAW			
Private practice			
Associate	58,942	74,318	103,562
Partner	114,213	183,364	301,611
Public prosecutor	23,000	30,000	38,000
Public defender	20,000	28,900	40,000
Corporate lawyer	61,932	79,297	111,708

Profession	Initial Pay	Industry Average	Typical Top Pay
Chief legal officer	169,300	258,966	445,000
Paralegal	30,470	37,686	50,544
LOBBYING			
Trade association lobbyist			
Small trade group	35,000	47,500	60,000
Large trade group	100,000	300,000	500,000
Corporate lobbyist	36,000	60,000	120,000
MANUFACTURING			
Foreman	32,240	40,300	48,360
Purchasing agent	42,240	52,800	63,360
Warehouse manager	41,231	53,600	65,969
Director of engineering	57,231	74,400	91,569
Manager of materials	57,308	74,500	91,692
Plant manager	77,462	100,700	123,938
VP for manufacturing	106,231	138,100	169,969
MARKETING			
Marketing assistant	18,900	24,000	30,000
Market research manager	45,770	57,000	103,000
Brand manager	45,000	61,000	109,125
Direct-marketing manager	40,000	66,000	110,000
VP for marketing	109,250	146,050	212,750
MEDIA			
Newspaper reporter	21,856	24,127	37,113
Magazines			
Senior editor	28,800	41,900	76,000
Managing editor	28,400	44,000	210,000
Executive editor	43,100	52,800	443,000

Profession	Initial Pay	Industry Average	Typical Top Pay
Book editor	21,000	44,090	72,990
TV news reporter	16,560	30,400	92,688
TV news anchor	25,453	65,824	248,183
Movie producer	400,000	1,000,000	5,000,000
Movie director	50,000	300,000	500,000
MIDDLE MANAGEMENT	50,035	69,675	151,165
PUBLIC RELATIONS			
Publicity agent	19,210	49,877	66,467
In-house publicist	23,400	55,480	62,613
SALES			
Sales trainee	19,800	30,700	35,400
Sales representative	38,900	48,400	59,900
Sales manager	55,800	65,300	80,300
District sales manager	64,900	74,800	88,100
Regional sales manager	81,400	95,000	116,400
VP for sales	136,100	178,200	226,900
SECRETARIES			
Secretary	12,480	28,189	50,000
Receptionist	13,000	22,387	28,000
Executive secretary	14,000	37,485	70,000
WALL STREET			
Investment banker			
Generalist	95,000	440,000	1,250,000
M&A specialist	95,000	590,000	1,750,000
Trader			
General instruments	60,000	290,000	1,000,000
Foreign exchange or derivatives specialist	60,000	360,000	2,000,000

Profession	Initial Pay	Industry Average	Typical Top Pay
Risk manager	450,000	725,000	1,000,000
Retail stockbroker	50,000	150,000	620,000
Institutional stockbroker	88,000	345,000	1,000,000

After carefully reviewing this list, you'd do well to look toward professions where the "industry average" or at least the "typical top pay" category gets to $100K. Of course, lots of jobs require you to work your way up, therefore starting lower. But even if you reach the top of your profession, if it's one that according to the statistics doesn't pay $100K, it's probably never going to pay six figures no matter how much you excel in it.

According to census reports of people earning over $100K:

- 89% are men.
- 91% are white.
- 81% are married.
- 9% are divorced or separated.
- 8% have never been married (2 percent are widowed).
- 49% have postgraduate or professional degrees.
- 31% have only a bachelor's degree.
- 12% have only some college.
- 8% have a high school diploma or less

(Interesting note: People with four years of college almost double earnings of people with four years of high school.)

You must take the time, make the commitment, and be eager to grow—to work on past skills, current skills, and skills needed for future earning capacity.

People like to say a salary is just a way of keeping score. Staying with that analogy, why not keep your own score today? Every time you catch yourself doing something well, stick a dollar in a special place. If you really miss some opportunities to practice these traits, take a dollar out. Don't count the kitty until the end of the month. By my calculation, there could be a few hundred dollars in there. Use it as reward money for you and the people who helped make it happen.

There are endless ways to make it into the $100K Club. Bullrider Tuff Hedeman says, "In order to ride bulls, you have to focus and concentrate on what it takes to make a good ride." That's what we are doing when we examine the traits of those who excel in any profession. In the next three chapters, let's look at the specific differences in skills required to excel in a corporate job and in a self-employed entrepreneurial situation.

"Pick the right rodeo and when you get on, give it a hundred and ten and you'll get in the money."

—JEROME DAVIS,
Championship Bullrider
(Archdale, North Carolina)

"One must have not only balance but integration. Balance implies a separation of business and personal which means a disruption of thought to action; a diversion of creative flow. Integration combines business with personal and daily activities. One focus refreshes and invigorates the other."

—LYNN BUTKUS,
President, Butkus
Consulting

"Make yourself invaluable to the company, either by the knowledge you have accumulated about the industry you're in (or the product you make), by the critical experience you've developed within the company, or by the strategic role you play. Become a key employee, one whose role directly impacts the company's future."

JIM FITZHENRY,
General Counsel, Flir Systems,
Inc.

CHAPTER 4

Making a Six-Figure Income in a Corporate Environment

"A six-figure corporate job is a twenty- to thirty-year bet. Not everyone ends up winning," says Ernie Howell, a retired CEO. "There is some luck involved."

In a large company you can work hard all your life, and without a little good luck, little happens. It's not as critical as the luck required in winning the lottery. (As Fran Lebowitz describes that kind of chance, "I figure you have the same chance of winning the lottery whether you play it or not.") Success in corporate America requires more than luck and it is more controllable than any lottery. But sometimes it is not that far off either.

A lot of people find out that joining—and gambling on—a big company turns out to be a poor hand. *Unless* they decide to really play the corporate game. The corporate game is not a bad thing, by the way. It's just the best way to describe an activity that has rules, requirements, competition, goals, and, yes, winners and losers.

This chapter is about playing the corporate game well. If you play well and have some additional favorable luck, you may also end up breaking into the $100K Club.

At the tops of many corporations there are only so many chairs at the table. In a typical big company, for example, roughly two hundred people out of ten thousand employees are over the $100K mark.

At Pepsi-Cola, for example, out of approximately 46,000 employees:

- 500 make $90K plus 20 percent bonus with $40K in stock options.
- 156 make $105K plus 30 percent bonus with $125K in stock options.
- 46 make $150K plus 40 percent bonus and $250K in stock options.

That's only 702 people who are six-figure income earners in the company—an organization known for good pay.

As discussed in the previous chapter, more enter than excel in any route. That is particularly true in a corporate environment.

While I was writing this book, a business friend inquired, "What chapter are you on?"

"How to make $100K in a corporate environment," I said.

"Is embezzlement in there?" he asked.

His humorous inquiry made a point. Truth is, illegal dealings can make big money in companies. It constantly amazes me how many people try it. Some recent examples:

- A sales manager at a computer-manufacturing company shipped bricks in boxes marked HARDWARE to bogus clients to increase his sales volume.
- A national hotel chain's chief financial officer deposited hundreds of thousands of dollars into his own banking account.
- A professional moving-company driver stocked a warehouse full of "lost" office and household furniture that he later sold through a side business.
- An executive director of a national fund-raising organization illegally pocketed nearly $100K of fund-raising money, in addition to writing off expenses for a mistress's apartment.

All of these activities went unnoticed for a long time before those involved were caught. According to a security expert I talked with, a lot more goes on that is not caught.

Embezzlement is one way to get into the $100K Club. It will likely get you into jail as well. It is obviously *not* an approach recommended in this book.

It is a fact, though, that a lot of illegal activity gets missed in a corporate environment. Since the illegal actions I just mentioned aren't always noticed, you can understand why all of your positive actions aren't always noticed either!

One of the biggest (honest) mistakes employees make is assuming that good work will get noticed—and rewarded. Wrong. It rarely happens that easily. You have to perform super-effectively at your job as well as get the task noticed in subtle but certain ways. That's the corporate game.

While you have one direct boss, your boss has multiple direct reports—plus a boss of his own. Many dynamics are going on simultaneously: projects, departments, divisions, groups, teams. People up and down the line have their own personal career agendas (like you do) in addition to work objectives.

A lot is going on in an organization, so naturally a lot can get missed. To repeat: In order to make $100K in a corporation, you must be doing superior—not just good—work in your job. And you can't let your successful efforts go unnoticed. You have to let the right people know.

To make a six-figure income in a corporate job, there are three things you need to do:

- Quantify your contributions and make sure the right people know about them.
- Accept the fact of office politics.
- Work in a profit center.

Quantify Your Contributions and Make Sure the Right People Know About Them

You have to achieve what the company sets as goals for you. Be methodically self-disciplined in your work and on your job. You can achieve those goals in a methodical approach, or you can achieve them some other way, but you still need to make it appear as if it were a systematic approach. That's part of the corporate gamble.

Understand how things need to be done in your firm. Adapt to that structure.

Methodical means simple things in most companies: send memos, respond to E-mail, be prompt, return phone calls, be visible, get results. It is important how something—*anything*—is perceived in most any institution. It's image. It's pretty easy, though. To manage your image, ask questions and listen better than the next person. If you aren't mastering this, you haven't asked the right questions.

This reminds me of an ex-government forester I met. Her job was to determine which trees needed to be cut down at a national park. I asked, "How do you know which trees?" I was prepared for a technical response. She answered, "I listen to the tree and let it make the decision." If she can lend an ear to the tree and get an answer, surely you can listen to your manager.

Too many readers glide over the advice to ask questions because it seems like such an obvious thing to recommend. Even if it is obvious, it's still not done often enough. For good question-asking:

- Prepare the questions in advance.
- Ask them early on.
- Have courage to ask the question that may appear dumb.
- Get lots of people involved.
- Take recesses to think of new questions.
- Be quiet after listening.
- Ask some questions that you already have the answer for.
- Give information.
- Stimulate thought with add-ons.
- Provide closure to the subject.

Do you always consider the items in this list when trying to catch on to the company arrangement? Probably not. *This is your job, you know!* To excel in your job, you have to understand what means success to your employer. To understand, you must ask questions—at the beginning of the conversation, in the middle, and before the end.

Be careful, though. Poorly executed questions can antagonize or, worse, challenge someone's honesty. If you ask without consideration of timing, ask merely to show off how smart you are, or use questions to cancel out someone else's questions—that's doing a bad job.

Also, don't be asking questions when you:

- Haven't paid attention
- Are revealing your ignorance
- Forgot the conversation
- Haven't formulated the question well
- Might embarrass others
- Aren't listening, only preferring to talk

"Truth is, twenty-five percent of corporate memos are CYA [meaning 'Cover Your Ass']," says John Krebs, president of Parker Company. Inquiring helps you find out which part of your *A* you have to *C*.

A major requirement of working within your corporate environment is to turn opportunities into contributions—and then let superiors know about it in a palatable manner. How do you make sure which contributions are valued by your manager and the company? You ask. Ask early and often. Then: ***Quantify your contributions and make sure the right people know about them.***

If people don't share the good things they're doing, "it's an issue of value missed," Mark Wheless, an executive vice president of Pepsi-Cola, explained to me. "I like to know the good things people are doing so I can help them take it further, or I can learn something to reapply. Regardless of the reason, if people don't share it, their contribution may be missed. . . . Let's not forget why we're here. The one reason is contribution. Otherwise, everyone loses. Starting at the $100K level, value added is needed big time."

Too often in a corporate setting people whine and act

like their employer owes them more—yet these are the same people *not* giving 110 percent.

What could possibly be the harm in contributing too much, anyway, giving more than your share?

"They'll take advantage of me!" you might say.

So what? You control how long you let that happen. Besides, if you're doing the work of two or three people, I guarantee your company's competitor will find out about it and some headhunter will snap you up for a client who will reward you.

The more likely result of doing too much is that you will experience your boss as:

- Increasingly loyal
- Less price-sensitive when it comes to salary negotiation
- Not inclined to shop around for someone else
- More likely to look to you for expertise in other areas
- Helpful in dramatically improved performance appraisals
- Willing to include you in his planning and forecasting
- Willing to introduce you to others; likely to send his friends and associates your way

A few things to keep in mind as you quantify your contributions:

Don't Be Lazy About This

You know the meaning of *lazy:* The habit of slowing down and resting before you get tired doing it!

Remember when I wrote about how many good and bad activities go undetected because so much is going on at the same time in any vital organization? That is why it is important for you to keep at it (by asking questions) so you can check yourself (as others can) about your worth to the organization.

Sometimes people think it is nobly modest and humble not to make an effort to get their work noticed by the right people. That's *one* perspective. Another one is that it is being lazy.

In the last chapter I pointed out a significant difference between those who merely enter a job and those who excel—those who excel do more. Only 10 percent more helps! So all I'm asking is for you to do your exemplary work and then put some of the extra 10 percent effort into *showing* your value and worth.

Let people know by volunteering straight information:

- "My team did . . ."
- "The results of our work are . . ."
- "Here are the steps we took to get . . ."

(Note: Notice the use of *we* versus *I*? Share the credit upward and downward.)

Don't Use Buzzwords

You know the ones: *paradigm shift, change agent, helicoptering, headlighting, dial up, adhocracy,* or adding *ize* to create your own word: *informationalize, imaginize, customerize.*

Too often buzzwords are used by technical people to frighten the boss, or sometimes to make others feel dumb. These words limit your universality, hamper creativity, and minimize your ability to say what you really mean.

Buzzwords make you look like you are trying to "talk the talk" rather than "walk the walk." Plus you look silly.

Words are everything in life. They calm fears, resolve conflict, ignite groups, and destroy relationships. Watch your choice of words.

Use candor rather than clichés.

Display Confidence

You exhibit confidence when you: air problems rather than hide them, get to the point instead of being long-winded, communicate face-to-face and by phone rather than only sending letters or faxes, and, as just mentioned, use *we* instead of *I.*

Be aware that no one wants to see, hire, or work with

someone who is nervous. If you appear apprehensive about your endeavors, why should anyone have confidence in you?

People you see and admire at the senior executive level aren't confident all of the time. Few can be sure of their results in every situation. Frequently they have to act confident while reporting their results to inspire others to do good work. Sometimes you'll have to do that also.

Don't Go Around Your Boss (Unless It Is Absolutely *the Last Resort)*

If you have a boss who won't listen or reward your ideas and contributions, it is still a mistake to go around him or her, at least early on. Keep working on the individual from different directions. Exhaust all your other options before going around.

A few companies, like Hewlett-Packard, have an open-door policy in which employees can go up the chain of command until they get their issues addressed. That's fine as long as you also use that open door to turn around and compliment or otherwise acknowledge good work. People forget that this part of the open door is like a bank account. Before you can make hefty withdrawals, you'd better make hefty deposits. If you never praised a manager and then you go around her, don't expect much support.

There is a length of time during which you must stay in place and wait before going around your boss, and it is generally longer than you'd like. When the time has been stretched to the limit and you conclude you have no option, accept the fact that going around your direct manager could end up a win for you but it will likely be a loss for him. Therefore, it *might* ultimately be a loss for you too.

You have three alternatives here: Get someone else to go around for you, move out from under that boss, or wait forever.

This is where your need for balance of your alls from Chapter 2 comes into play. If you've spent time every day putting effort into the people and interests that make up your alls, you have someone or something that might provide the key that allows you to reach someone higher up or around your immediate boss.

I recall a client who needed an audience with the "big" boss but there was no way he had an entrée. As luck would have it, however, the client's weekend fun job was training amateur pilots to fly small aircraft. Who should be his weekend student one trip, but the "big" boss! Amazing luck!

By the way, show appreciation for support you do get from any level and don't force obligations. Forcing obligations only works temporarily.

Initiate a Quarterly (At Least) Meeting with Your Manager

Do it in a formal setting, not casually over a beer. Go through a self-appraisal process and say, "These are the things I've done and I'm ready for my next step. Tell me what I have to do in your eyes to do that." If he says, "Four more years at blankety-blank," you have basically two choices:

- Agree with him and go fix what needs to be fixed.
- If you feel it is unattainable, pleasantly say, "I don't like it." Ask if there is a workable way around this. If not, you may need to get out altogether or move to another division of the company.

There may come a time when you no longer have the choice to sit back and wait for your higher-ups to take the time and effort to quantify your worth.

Most people who have taken the initiative and left an employer have told me, "In retrospect, I wish I'd left earlier."

Ed, a regional computer engineering department manager, chose to leave. Some months later I was surprised to see him in coveralls, crawling around a client's floor doing electrical work. Eight years later I saw him again, still as an electrician, driving a brand-new pickup truck. "I'm the happiest I've ever been in my life," he told me. "I don't know what I was doing at the computer company. Thank God I got out."

Since you likely have to complete performance appraisal forms on your subordinates, here's a suggestion: Throughout the month, whenever you notice one of your people doing something particularly well (or poorly) note it on a three-by-five card and put it in your file on the employee. It will make for easier and more specific reviews, plus it helps in evaluating pay increases and promotions. Without the concrete comparison among people, too many decisions are pure "gut." (Do the same thing for yourself when you do something particularly well.)

Then take this a step further. Since your boss is probably not doing this for you, you have to make note of your accomplishments for yourself. That's where the periodic checks with questions become valuable: You're letting the right people know what you're up to and hearing whether they like it or not!

Be Resilient

It is easy to get discouraged in the corporate world. There are so many people and factors intent on your submission and failure. Keep faith in yourself. Accept the fact that your job is to work in the system, not change the system. Don't give up on the structure or yourself.

NBC News reported on a survey of how employees react to criticism and setbacks from their boss:

- 40 percent talk about it behind the boss's back.
- 23 percent have a passive reaction (whatever that means).
- 19 percent provide less productive work.
- 17 percent yell at the boss.
- 3 percent get physical.

Be flexible and resilient. Bend more. Adapt to your environment. (That does not mean compromise.) Cooperate. One recruiter told me, "*Everyone* has to change to be successful in any specific company." So it's not just you and I who have to!

On a San Francisco street corner I saw a panhandler with a sign, NONAGGRESSIVE PANHANDLER. I walked by, but it intrigued me so much I went back to him and asked, "Do you get more money with the sign?" He looked at me, surprised that I'd asked and said, "Yeah." I responded, "I was just wondering," and I started walking away. He spoke up, wanting to tell me more: "I was listening to the mayor talk on the news and he said tourists don't like aggressive panhandlers, so I made up this sign." He continued, "I don't like it when people harass me on the street. And the sign makes people smile. You have to have a sense of humor in this line of work." I laughed and put a dollar in his can. He'd earned it because he understood the system.

Follow the Company Line

The company is your employer. The company does pay your salary. As long as there is legal, ethical behavior, adhere to the company line.

There are frequent headlines about one company or another full of graft. It does happen. But it is a small percent of the total group of corporations out there. It makes news because it is rare.

I understand the company line can seem unfair, distasteful, unpleasant, unkind. There are always at least two sides to every situation. For your survival (and sanity) look for the positive, productive, constructive perspective. I'm not saying dogmatically accept it; but at least look carefully at the other side before attacking the easily obvious.

An interesting different perspective of taking the company line: The cost of accepting the company line *to the company* is that they lose some of their employees' imagination. They also lose some spontaneity, plus a lot of talent goes to waste. People become a little timid when they just follow their orders.)

Accept the fact that, in a corporate environment, things aren't done in a high-performance manner all of the time. Understand you have to achieve results in an acceptable way.

This reminds me of the advice I heard on a song while flipping channels on the radio: "Don't be original, it's been done before."

Find Out How Your Job Fits into the Whole Picture

In a big corporation, jobs tend to get cut into very small pieces and seldom do you get to see the whole picture. You must change that for yourself. Work (and ask) to see how your piece fits into the whole. Take the initiative to find out. You're at risk when you *don't* know where your contribution fits for the big picture. (Remember the importance of building a case for yourself—this may be the foundation block.)

A task chart can be drawn like an organization chart. Plot out where pieces fit together in the whole: Sketch squares around projects, draw dotted and solid lines between projects and people. Have your boss draw a task chart to see if you two are thinking the same. Plus you can re-ask a few months down the road to see how things have changed.

This exercise puts things into perspective.

When I use the expression "put things into perspective," I always remember the time many years ago when I had just treated myself to the purchase of a red Porsche 911-SC convertible. Literally, the first time I took it for a drive on a sunny day with the car top down, a pigeon made a deposit on my shoulder. Sometimes outside sources can really put things into perspective for you.

Become an Expert

If you have everything you need for success except success, you have yet to be known as an expert. Be the ace on your team, in your office, company, city, state, industry, country, whatever. It only requires attitude and activity on your part. You may have to give speeches, volunteer for task forces, speak at meetings, and so on. (You know, that 10 percent extra!)

A key area to become an expert in—in addition to some technical areas—is understanding your boss. Let me clue you in to what bosses want, in addition to good work: They want to feel good about themselves, feel what they do matters, and be recognized for good judgment by their peers and their own bosses.

Like most people, they want to avoid potential risk or trouble, avoid insecurity that comes from surprises and changes, and avoid being boxed in both now and in the future. Good bosses want to meet their personal goals without violating their integrity. Naturally, they want good explanations, to be told the truth, and to be thought of as honest and fair. Most want to be liked and treated nicely.

They want to work easier, not harder—and they want to keep their job and get promoted.

That list of what bosses want sounds pretty much like what you want, doesn't it?

So far, we've discussed what you do personally. Now let's look at what you do with the rest of the people with whom you work.

Accept the Organizational Dance as a Fact of Office Politics

Without the ability to deal with the people and politics at work, you will fall.

According to *Roget's Thesaurus,* the first synonym listed for *politics* is "statesmanship." This synonym puts a whole new spin on it, right? President Clinton's former adviser George Stephanopoulos, famous for being a spin doctor, explains spinning as just putting a positive twist on a situation. That's what you have to do on the corporate playing field regarding your "statesmanship opportunities."

In any company with more than one person, there is not a question of whether office politics exists or not. The questions are only how entrenched, at what levels, how deeply, for good or bad, and where do and can I fit in. Plainly and simply, you *have* to operate within the political culture.

People bemoan, complain, and whine about the political side of an organization. Heck, your own family has its own version of office politics. It is just human relationships.

In statesmanship, as in your personal life, you need balance. The key is what action, with whom, and when it needs to be done.

When people are always looking at everybody else, that's office politics. When you look at yourself, that's *managing* office politics. Like the Hank Williams, Jr., song goes. "If you mind your own business, you'll be busy all of the time . . . and you won't be mindin' mine."

If you view politics as a negative that necessitates compromise and cunning, then that is not a good thing. If you see politics as a positive force requiring you to be aware of and sensitive to others, enthuse them to your point of view, and be able to read others, without compromise and cunning, that is a good thing.

Office politics is simply how you do what you do:

- Getting the promotion you think you deserve over the person who also thinks she deserves it is office politics.
- Doing your work with a relaxed smile so you appear to be having a good time at your work is office politics.
- Loaning some of your people to another manager who needs assistance to meet his objectives and therefore look good to his boss is office politics.

One computer project manager said to me, "I was told by my boss that because I came in with the answers, I made my team members look bad. And that having the right answer wasn't the thing to do—that I needed to work on not intimidating people." That's also office politics.

To become a $100K Club member in corporate America, you must be extraordinarily gifted politically and astute in getting through the system. This does not discount the substance side of your work.

Sometimes you will get rewarded for the fine job you do; often you will get rewarded just for your ability to get around in the corporate landscape and culture, working through the players in the way *they* want things done. Do not proclaim, "That's not my job." Wrong. In a corporate environment, office politics is part of your job—a big part.

Every company is different, so know the power source.

To write this book, I talked with men and women who have worked successfully in both corporate environments and self-employed entrepreneurial situations, to hear from them what they felt it took to do well. The overwhelming majority stated that the need to maneuver through the ranks is critical.

I'm defining office politics as the ability to deal with people in the following manner:

- Get along with them.
- Coordinate efforts through teamwork.
- Get a group to work toward one goal.
- Make friends.
- Neutralize enemies.
- Build relationships, associations, and alliances.

I repeat: This is not a bad thing if done without a hidden agenda, power plays, disingenuity, compromise, cheating, and other negative action and intent, particularly toward those who can't defend themselves.

Some refer to this activity as the science of kissing up. That is not what I am promoting. As I wrote previously, you should recognize the list as exactly what you do with your friends and family—get along, coordinate, work together toward a goal, minimize hurt and misunderstanding, and generally build relationships. The activity is no different, just attitudes toward it.

In business, maintain the outlook that supports the positive side of politics. If you do, you'll do well. If you don't, you won't do well. The negative side will consume you and block your way to earning $100K.

So how do you become more politically astute, since success in the company depends on it? Here are recommendations from $100K Club members to help you do it right:

- Be keenly aware and constantly observe.
- Go out and meet new people.
- Be accessible yourself.
- Look to provide the boss with more than sitting at your desk doing a job.
- Build a network.
- Know what positively triggers people around you.
- Hold your tongue.

Be Keenly Aware and Constantly Observe

Keep your eyes and ears open. From day one, watch and listen to who talks to whom, about what, and when.

You don't have to do what they do, you just have to know who is doing what.

One head of a television network described the complicated surroundings his people work in: "It takes six months to find out where the bathrooms are, much less how things operate."

Even if you've been with a group a long time, start anew today to retune in to what is going on. Put away your biases about what should and shouldn't be and who is and isn't a good person. Try to be as clear and open in your observation as if you just started in that company. (By the way, it *is* as if you just started in the company if you haven't been doing this all along.)

Know the company drill—the ins and outs—so well, you become irreplaceable.

Go Out and Meet People

Do not wait until others—up or down the levels of authority—come to you. Go to them.

True, it is flattering if people go out of their way to introduce themselves to you, perhaps pay a compliment on your good work, or observe something of interest to you. Since it is fun to receive that attention, why not be the giver of it, so someone else gets the fun? Don't second-guess what you might gain with someone if you do it. That turns into craftiness, not building alliances.

The people you should make an effort to meet are the ones you are most uncomfortable with. (It's easy to meet the likable, approachable ones. Anybody can do that.) The difficult ones are your targets.

Our sixteenth president, Abe Lincoln, knew this simple fact. He once said, "I don't like that man, I must get to know him better."

Be Accessible Yourself

I can recall one male client who was sent to me for consulting from a packaging company, and his boss's biggest complaint was, "I can never find him. He's always with customers, doing a good job, but I need to know what it is."

Although the boss was certainly pleased the subordinate had good customer relations, to the boss it was just as important to be kept aware of activities so she could speak intelligently and in an informed manner to *her* boss. Always needing to track him down made it look like the supervisor had no control over what her people were doing.

Look to Provide Your Boss with More *than Sitting at Your Desk Doing a Job*

Work to produce a little extra something for people to benefit from and see. (Yes, that's right, you have to make sure people see what you've done.)

A $200K-plus member described his approach: "Too many people settle for good enough. I don't. If I get a three on a performance appraisal, I don't ask, 'How did that happen?' I ask, 'What do I need to get to a four? And how about a five?' Whatever the company needs, I'm going to make sure it gets."

I'm sure you aren't ever a do-nothing type of person, but I want to make sure you also aren't a do-a-little-bit type either. Remember, it may only take an additional 10 percent.

Build a Network

You are going to see the same faces, a lot, for a long amount of time; you might as well build relationships.

If you have a good idea on how to sell the company's product but you only know the manufacturing manager, she's likely not going to help you much. If you build a network of people, you can work with them to get to the marketing manager.

Links are necessary inside and outside of your company and industry—on and off the job.

One data-processing manager complained to me, "You lose out on half the business conference if you don't put a golf club in your hand." Instead of taking that situation literally, take it figuratively: Unless you participate in activities outside of the direct mainstream of business, you will miss out on the multidimensions of a person, his personality, and his interests. (By the way, I know plenty of six-figure income earners who don't play golf. Playing that particular game isn't the point. The point is taking on *some* activity that helps you build and maintain a network.)

Think about yourself. If you followed the advice in Chapter 2 and are constantly working on developing your all, then there is more to you than this money-earning machine. You hunt or fish or golf. You have children. You crochet. You built your own house. You . . . on and on. You are a multidimensional person. And it is human nature to want to share this with others. That's building a network.

I know a man who has made his own wine for years since going to college in Paris. He acknowledges he got hired into a company because his new boss was starting to make wine and he wanted a personal in-house consultant.

You don't have to take up golf (unless you want to). But you do have to find common interests to share with those you work with, if you want to bond with them. Try dinner or lunch as a start. Then maybe you'll end up at the same cultural event or political function.

Remember, as well, not to exclude others who don't share those same interests. (And obviously, don't let them exclude you either.)

Know What Positively *Triggers People Around You*

Keenly understand their interests. My previous book, *How to Think Like a CEO* (Warner Books, 1996), is subtitled *The 22 Vital Traits You Need to Be the Person at the Top*. I analyzed CEOs to see what they have that allows them to do their jobs. Obviously, the traits they possess are significant to their success. That's knowing what positively triggers people around you.

The 22 vital traits displayed by CEOs:

1. They are secure in themselves.
2. They are in control of their attitude.
3. They are tenacious.
4. They are constantly improving.
5. They are honest and ethical.
6. They think before speaking.
7. They are original.
8. They are modest in public.
9. They are aware of style.
10. They are gutsy, even a little wild.
11. They have a sense of humor.
12. They are a tad theatrical.

13. They are detail-oriented.
14. They are good at their job and are willing to lead.
15. They fight for their people.
16. They are willing to admit mistakes, yet are unapologetic.
17. They are straightforward.
18. They are nice.
19. They are inquisitive.
20. They are competitive.
21. They are flexible.
22. They are good storytellers.

Hold Your Tongue

When the boss is spouting B.S., you can't get up and say, "That's B.S." That restraint takes self-control. It's sort of like one financial man who said to me: "Debra, you see me as five-foot-ten. I'm really six-five. I'll go back to my original height when I get this boss off my back with his stupidity."

In the corporate arena you can't be flippant. You can't be brash, too persistent, or go after things in an aggressive way—if it isn't the company's way. (And in most companies it isn't.) Somebody above you will undoubtedly remember it.

Don't allow yourself to say whatever you want to—or say it because you believe it to be true. You wouldn't do that at home with someone you love; you shouldn't do it on the job with someone you work with.

"Hold your tongue" doesn't mean refrain from saying something sensitive and significant; it means rephrase or reframe that something.

So: Why bother with office politics?

One, to avoid being fired. One friend of mine described his departure from his corporate marketing job: "After they fired me, I was escorted out the front door with a security guard on each arm."

Two, to be a web climber. Not the information web of life today, but the spiderweb of business: the interconnections, cross-overs, overlaps, crisscross of people and information up and down and sideways. Some people build webs to trap people. That is not what I mean. I want you to be a person who sees all the dimensions and can maneuver in and around the web.

Three, to be the one the deals are done with. ABC and Disney took eight days to do a $19 billion merger, according to Disney CEO Michael Eisner. That took strategic partnerships that came from being politically astute.

Business gets done fast and profitably through good office statesmanship.

Now, before you dismiss me as being naive about the destructive, damaging, powerful, harmful, unfair world of office politics, let me say: *I know.* Why do you think I'm self-employed? I couldn't stand it.

Companies say they want creativity, risk-taking, and entrepreneurial skills. However, that isn't rewarded. What is rewarded is politicking with the right people.

I can recall a meeting of top managers of a company discussing their reorganization. Many millions had been misappropriated, illegal activities had rocked the foundation, Wall Street and the public was extremely leery about the company. Discussions about the "new" way of doing business, though, centered on the just-hired "players," the change of floors, and office redecoration! One of the new players told me, "Going in, I thought the organization was about seventy percent political. I was wrong. It's one hundred percent."

I asked the fired marketing manager I mentioned in an earlier example, "How do companies survive getting work done if so much time is spent in negative office politics?" He said, "When I worked for X company [a soap manufacturer] I used to think there was a guy in the basement of our office towers making soap supporting the entire twelve floors above him. The low-level workers, people in the field, provide the profit. The hierarchical levels are going along and getting along despite themselves. Once the system is set up, it just keeps moving. It's a bureaucratic power game that feeds itself on the people who can't defend themselves."

So, let me repeat: I don't deny the destructive potential of business maneuvering. I do know there are thousands of famous, fabulous executives in corporate America who got there because they are not only good, but good statesmen too. They:

- Get along with people
- Coordinate efforts through teamwork

- Get a group to work towards a goal
- Make friends
- Neutralize enemies
- Build relationships, associations, and alliances

Now for the big mistakes to avoid when dealing with the political side of work: Avoid fearing office politics, concentrating exclusively on them, being intimidated by those more proficient, making a mistake because of that fear, trying too hard to be liked, assuming you know what others want, feeling too shy to insert (and assert) yourself, and minimizing the importance of office politics.

A reasonable way to look at beneficial office politics is: doing the right thing, at the right time, for the right reason—with the right people.

Here are some specific actions $100K Club members take regarding their office politics management.

- Share information when it's fresh with someone you might not normally share with (even if she doesn't share with you).
- Ask when something is unclear; never assume anything—check it out immediately.
- Brag about others in front of others.
- Make an effort to stay in contact with people after the team has dismantled or they have left the company.
- Be reliable. Do what you say you will, when you say you will, on time, right, the first time.

- Service your co-workers and boss as you would a customer.
- Be credible, safe, and dependable in the little things as well as the big ones.
- Help co-workers with their work.
- Be empathetic. Make your co-workers feel special. Basically treat them the way you'd like to be treated in the same situation.
- Communicate in, rather than dominate, a conversation.
- Write down complaints, problems, frustrations, then put that aside and review it later.
- Notice that most every situation gets better when you do.

Now, with all of this said, let me add one very important thing. When you are playing this game of politics, *be in a profit center* in the company. Nothing else matters quite as much. If you aren't in a revenue-producing segment of the company, then you need to do all of the things just listed expertly just to keep a job, much less get more money for it. To get more money, a person has to be able to concretely show his contribution to the dollar value of the company.

That means produce revenue, don't count revenue; get in operations, not administration.

Pay is based on either how much you *personally* contribute to the organization or how you affect another's contribution. A scientist and a manager might get paid the same because one is the contributor (the scientist) and one gets others to contribute (the manager)—but they both add revenue.

People only pay you if they have to.

Why should anyone pay you at all? To keep you. To reward you. To motivate your performance. You have to be worth keeping, rewarding, and motivating. Charm, looks, lineage, and shimmy and shake don't cut it. Charging hard with smarts, discipline, and creativity does.

Now, you could be saying to me right now: "Hey, I know and do all of these things, but I still can't get over the $60, or $70, or $80, or $90K level. What gives?"

I realize that does happen, probably far too often, so let's talk about getting over the hurdle.

Corporate Salaries

Suppose you have documented evidence of your financial value to the company, have quantified your accomplishments, developed political skills, and are at the point where you think you should be getting more money. Check your assumptions against these questions:

- How long have you been in the job and in the company?

- How recent was the last move up?
- Are you keeping up with or ahead of people who have a comparable grade and longevity with the company?
- Where are your peers, subordinates, and superiors?
- Are you seen as on the track for promotion?
- What is your worth to the company?
- What is your worth in the marketplace?

The answers should be such that an objective third party (not your spouse or in-laws) would draw the conclusion: "Deserves a raise."

Now try to come up with an honest, clear evaluation of the issues that your company's management considers regarding your pay and possible increases. The factors they measure against are:

- *Qualifications.* Your education and experience in the field.
- *Nature and scope of the work.* What do you do that is crucial to the company.
- *Size and complexity of business.* Often this is compared to competitors.
- *Salary versus total income.* Bonuses, catch-up bonuses, club, fees, et cetera.
- *Economic conditions.* Declining prices and heavy competition.
- *Salary policy.* Long-standing, consistent compensation plans.
- *Financial condition.* Very profitable or not.

- *Comparable pay.* Compared to other similar companies.
- *Previous year's pay.*

A simple example: The compensation of a CFO in a twenty-person company as opposed to a CFO of a $200 million company is going to have considerably different measurements.

Now, I caution you, despite all the objective analysis, when the subject of money comes up, there will be more than one boss whose response is "No can do, no want do, no will do," no matter what. You must work to get out from under that boss.

Before you erroneously conclude that is *your* boss, try to get your pay increased anyway. You may surprise yourself and succeed, and at the very least you'll get practice to help you with a next boss.

How? From day one with your boss, ask, "Did I meet your expectations? Where could I have done better?"

When I suggest daily, I don't mean becoming an irritating pest regarding the subject. You have to be subtle (which you know how to do because of your statesmanlike abilities). But you must constantly verify you're on track. If you do this as a matter of your regular work style, bosses will come to expect it and more readily and clearly provide the feedback. If you try it once a year at the performance appraisal session, you haven't trained them to respond effectively for you.

Some sample questions in addition to "Did I meet your expectations?" could be:

- "Next time we tackle this type of problem, what would you like to see done differently?"
- "What about our approach on the _________ situation? In your opinion, what made it so successful?"
- "How have you handled _________ type of problems in the past?"
- "What advice would you give to a person like me on _________?"
- "Why do you think we have so many surprises while doing _________?"
- "Who could I talk to about better ways to deal with _________ in the future?"
- "Who should we let know about the successful outcome of _________?"
- "When we face this again, is there anything you want me to do differently?"
- "Where do you think we'll have the biggest obstacles in this next project? What can I do to minimize that happening?"

You notice the tone of the questions is productive, constructive, problem-solving. They are not asked with an insecure attitude or manner of, "Am I okay, did I do good, do you like me?"

You'll also notice they start with *who, what, when, where, why, how.* Those are the words reporters use to get to the facts and write the news. They will work for you to get to the facts also.

If you are hearing the answers that consistently and passionately say "good job, on track," then pay should be commensurate—at the market rate. Remember the market rate for the job you're in may never be over the $100K mark; you may be wasting your time *if* your job function never gets to that level. You may have to switch to a different function inside or outside of the company. The next chapter will be on job hunting, if that is the direction you need to take.

Above all, first do an exemplary job. As one recruiter put it, "Stop bitching about the money. Perform. Let people know you did. But first *perform.*"

If you perform, there is no reason your pay should be below market rate. Unless, one, you've made a conscious decision to be in a specific geographic location or industry that historically has paid and will likely continue to pay below market rate; or two, you've set your sights beyond your capability.

Too many times people read what I've just written and proclaim it unrealistic for the real world. I disagree. What would be unrealistic is people's emotional expectations without the solid basis of the daily dialogue I've recommended. What follows is an example of a woman—who will remain nameless, since she is still employed by the corporation—who did all of the objective analysis and it turned out exactly as she had hoped:

> I was head of training for a company that was acquired by my current employer. The new management didn't hold training in high regard. After a few months with the new organization, I put together a report that we had a

problem and, unless we dealt with it, we'd lose good people. I took it to my boss and after he read it he said, "I knew all that."

"You knew that and haven't taken action to change it?" I asked in amazement. "Well then, I'm out of here."

The senior management of the company found out about the report and my decision to leave and came to me with, "We're not letting you go. And we want you to be the new director" (the job of the man I'd given the report to). Since by that time I'd gotten another job offer, they agreed to meet the salary offer, thus a good pay increase, plus they said, "You'll be able to make a difference here from now on."

They lived up to their words.

In our company, like most, training is viewed as a necessary evil, not a strategic differentiator. But I pay attention to the details to see where my work does make a difference. After about ten months I went to my boss and said, "I'm doing this and this. . . . With my head count and responsibility I should be a vice president."

I could back it up, I'd made a defensible case, and I was confident. She agreed.

I also said, "I don't feel I'm equably compensated and that is not a good feeling." I hoped she understood, as I did, that the first step to someone considering leaving a job is they aren't feeling valued in their job. And not making comparable pay to other vice presidents made me *not* feel valued.

Her response: "You're right, we're looking into it."

The company promoted me with a pay increase that was retroactive!

Twelve months later I had to go in again. "I'm the second most profitable business unit in the company. I have the best customer satisfaction, I'm feeling disadvantaged because I'm left out of some meetings. I should be a senior vice president."

They did it.

Every time, I presented a solid case and felt confident in my position. I said things in a way that they could say no. If I had received a no, I would have asked, "What do I need to do?" If they couldn't satisfactorily explain what I needed to do, if they couldn't back up their decision about not giving me a promotion, I was prepared to leave and I'm sure they knew it.

Lots of time and effort on my part went into coming up with a strategy to approach them. I'd decide what to say, even writing down key phrases. And I tried to minimize any bumbling around in my requests due to the stress I was feeling.

What's the secret to my work success? I always take two extra seconds to pay attention to detail about all aspects of things. If you pay attention, you remember things.

It works everywhere. The car attendants at the Hertz counter know me because of those two extra seconds I give them—remembering their name, their daughter's name—they give me upgrades without me asking. It's what I use to set myself apart."

This senior vice president, who now makes $300K-plus, did nothing exceptional except: superior work, letting the right people know in an acceptable way, and being politically savvy while making clear requests. She had the courage to ask for what she deserved, but she also had the courage of her convictions to leave if requests weren't reasonably met.

If you've kept up the dialogue all of the time with the powers that be in your organization, it is easy to go in and ask, "How can I make more money? What additional responsibilities can I take on? Can you help me plan my career path?"

If the boss doesn't respond with specific, constructive responses—in other words, doesn't care if you progress or not—leave the company. To make six figures, you have to be risk-oriented and not risk-aversive.

Sometimes you only have two choices in making significantly more money: be patient and stay longer, or leave.

If you discover severe discrepancy in money, proceed deliberately, courageously, and, of course, with good common sense. If you get obsessed with the unfairness and go overboard in correcting the inequity, you may get what you want but make an enemy along the way. A communication chief gave a director the pay increase he relentlessly pursued. But instead of the $8,000 required to bring his pay up to par, he received $7,999, thus denying him a grade increase.

Set goals and chart your earnings. Traditionally an average performer could get a 5 percent annual raise. Today it's more likely to be 2.5 percent. A really good performer might get 10 percent. But if there is a big leap necessary to get up to market value, employers don't like to do it. Your history makes a difference. If you make $90K, they can justify a bump to $100K. If you are at $60K, you need to stair-step up, typically by going to a different company.

Before deciding to leave your employer, exhaust their "no" in pay options. If you're doing superb work (from an objective point of view) but policy prohibits the necessary percentage increase, ask about other incentives. Bonuses can be given for "catch-up," year-end, relocation, or other justifiable reasons. Profit sharing, management incentive programs, variable rewards, commissions, bonuses, and stock options all need to be explored as a way to bring your pay level up.

Robert Riggs is a company growth and compensation consultant in Fresno. I asked him to tell me about other compensation at the six-figure levels.

1. Financial category:

    - Financial planning assistance by a company-retained adviser
    - A personal insurance plan to pay the deductibles of the company-sponsored health and welfare plan
    - Elective insurance options such as additional life insurance, short-term disability, long-term disability, travel insurance for the executive, family, and spouse
    - Tuition savings plan
    - Estate planning services
    - International insurance such as hospitalization, especially emergency Medi-Vac (airplane or helicopter)
    - Company-paid financial portfolio management services
    - Entitlement to air miles

2. Recognition/prestige category:

    - Golf club membership
    - Resort membership
    - Access to company-owned vacation homes and the corporate jet
    - Company prestige credit card
    - Committee appointments (adviser to the board in the executive specialty)
    - Special project chairperson in the company, in the community, in the industry

- Governmental liaison (testimony before state agencies or the U.S. Congress, for example)
- Trade journal article written by the executive

3. Self-realization category:

- Sabbatical (with pay) for community service, education, family travel, writing a book, teaching
- Self-development/testing (Outward Bound type of school, for example)

One company's CEO has the philosophy of promoting people to the money of the next job level but without the title for a one-year trial period. Another company's policy is literally to look at the car the employee drives and house she lives in and arbitrarily decide whether she is making too much money or not! These aren't small companies with lax procedures. Both of these examples are from Fortune 500 organizations. Despite printed pay policies, bosses who truly want to can get around restrictions. Your job is to make your boss truly want to because of the value you provide him or her.

Bottom line: You have to be aggressive about proposing ways to increase your salary. Wanting it and feeling you justify it are insufficient. If you have a history of performance—plus can deliver even more—only then will you get your big move up with your current employer.

If your decision is to stair-step to another company, the next chapter will help you prepare and execute a hunt for six-figure jobs.

"In your day-to-day job, identify what you really need to focus on and how it evolves at different levels. Satisfy your boss and your boss's boss, no matter what.

"Exposure to senior people is usually limited, so every exposure counts no matter the situation or the environment. People who make key decisions about your career usually have a very limited number of impressions/interactions to form an opinion—accurate or not. Often group- and non-group-related interactions can leave the biggest impression. How you interact and how you say things is as important as what you say. Never underestimate how an impression is formed."

—KEN KUNZE,
Marketing Manager,
Rootbeer Beverage
Company

"1. You need to know the waterline your predecessor and counterparts set, then meet and exceed it all of the time.
"2. Teamwork is always important.
"3. Build confidence between peers and boss.
"4. Volunteer for hot assignments so you work

on things that continuously stretch your skill base.

"5. Consistently work on your own personal development; no one will ever be as interested in that as you."

—MINDY CREDI,
Human Resources
Director—California,
Pepsi-Cola Company

"Have a solid work ethic that you bring to the business. Take risks. You will fail at some. But it will tell you what you're made of.

"Develop a basic road map to achieve your target. Lay out the positions necessary and follow it even if it means changing companies or geographic location.

"Maintain a balanced patience. It won't happen overnight."

—BRIAN PIPER,
Director,
Dade International, Inc.

CHAPTER 5

How to Job Hunt at the $100K Level

If you are (or will soon be) on the street job hunting at the six-figure income level, you already know there are a limited number of the big jobs out there. In addition to the tedious, time-consuming, frequently frustrating experiences every other job hunter has, yours will be complicated with the limited choices available to you.

That's the bad news. The good news is . . .

If you are someone who believes in and subscribes to everything written so far in this book—balance your alls, do more than the next person, understand the world you work in, keep control of your career—you'll have no problem job hunting.

In fact, you'll enjoy it because it is fun to talk with a variety of people in different companies to learn what they are doing and see where it is you want to put your efforts for mutual success. Honestly, one $100K Club member said to me, "I'm having such a good time, I really hate to choose between the offers in front of me."

How you prepare yourself, how you approach looking for the $100K-plus job, and how you execute your plan needs the same strategy, effort, and creativity that you bring to a company in your job.

THE $100K CLUB JOB HUNT ATTITUDE ADJUSTMENT

Your approach toward the process will make—or break—your hunting success. The higher you go, the more important is mental attitude over mental capabilities. In the Olympics they call it sports psychology; in business it is career mental toughness. "Once we learn how to control our thoughts, we can be so much more than we already are," says psychologist James Millhouse.

The fact that 33 percent of employees fear losing their job (according to a *New York Times* poll) points out a poor attitude. *Not wanting* to lose your job is taking on a different and better perspective than *fearing* the loss of your job.

In truth, statistics prove that job insecurity outpaces

actual job loss. *Insecurity* is another word for poor attitude.

Out of 125 million people in the 1995 workforce, only 440,000 were laid off. The Labor Department reports that 75 percent of those fired workers got new jobs within two years. (Twenty-three weeks was the median search time.) Job loss is not as bad as the headlines read. If you have qualifications—and a managed attitude—there are new, better, and higher-paying jobs out there for you.

I know talk about positive attitude is old-hat advice. Nonetheless, all evidence points to it being the number one factor required for most jobs over $100K.

"My secretary screens résumés for people having the technical competence required. But when they get to me, the most important thing I look for is a positive attitude versus a 'woe is me' attitude," says Carolyn Rose, senior vice president of Novell.

The number one requirement for taking on a job hunt (whether you initiated it or not) is to *manage your perspective* about this life experience *all of the time.* The ancient Hawaiian warriors would go to the ocean every day before sunrise, walk into the water, and let the waves wash over them until all their bad attitudes or impure thoughts were purged. Daily, they mentally cleansed themselves.

That's what you must do daily during your job search. If you don't have an ocean to walk into, maybe a morning shower can do the same thing. But it needs to be done.

The president of U.S. Sprint-Canada, Bob Hansford,

says, "The toughest part in a search is maintaining a positive attitude."

With a positive, productive, constructive attitude, plan your $100K-plus job search strategy:

1. Define what you are competent to the core in. Review your alls to help you remember things important to you that were missing in the last job. Include those aspects in your next ideal job model. Don't try to be whatever is currently in demand in the marketplace; it will cause you to make poor decisions.

2. Put a lot of effort into identifying desirable companies. Look for the ones known for good pay. Try to spot organizations on the upswing—that is, those positioned to grow faster than their competitors. Look for ones undervalued by career seekers. Don't go for the trendy industries just because they are visible; they can take advantage of their popularity and pay less because their name will look good on someone's résumé. Search out organizations restructuring or at the bottom of a business cycle that aren't getting the press.

Even if you don't want to work overseas, the company should show signs of thinking globally. They aren't and won't be on the upswing if they don't understand the fast global marketplace.

Seek a company in which employees' personal lives are respected. In which mistakes are viewed as learning opportunities, not career suicide. And in which investment in their people is priority.

Look for a firm that values variety and allows flexibility in viewpoints, marketplaces, product lines, employees, approaches, and business in general. If they don't value diversity internally, they will never capture their market potential and you might not make the money you deserve.

How do you find all this out? Ask people in your circle of contacts and people they will introduce you to in *their* circle of contacts.

3. Produce some personal marketing tools that reflect where you've been, what you want, and where you're going. (Letters and résumés are discussed later in this chapter.)

4. Aim to have targeted companies hear about you four times before you approach them directly. They could learn about you through key employees, recruiters, industry publications, business journal "promoted" columns, community activities, speeches delivered, or name-dropping by centers of influence. Obviously this will take some time and effort, which brings us to Step 5.

5. Ideally, attack all of the preceding steps *before* you need a new job. But if you haven't and are in desperate straits to job hunt now, work on the preceding steps harder than you ever dreamed you possibly could.

6. Problems are certain to happen; try to enjoy them. View the setbacks, obstacles, and mistakes as good things because you'll know what not to do *next* time. If you don't learn anything from a loss, why lose? There is nothing wrong with losing except an outcome of giving up. (Consider the ex–regional director of Prudential Bache and ex–$100K Club member I know who now delivers telephone directories while moonlighting from his full-time pizza-delivery job.)

Fearing problems is a thing of the mind. If you don't offer fear a place to stay, it has none. That's attitude management.

Control your attitude, then do something constructive regarding the inevitable rejection:

- Get callused to it. There is a percentage of the population that will dislike you regardless of how good you are. Take heart in the fact that there will always be people who don't like the pope, the U.S. president, Miss America, even Big Bird.
- Never assume rejection before you actually get it. If you dread the potential no, potential employers will see it in your face, voice, and manner. You'll lose self-respect and get weaker in facing future obstacles.
- Get so good at work that you get less and less rejection. It's enough of a goal to get even *slightly* better *every* time you try something.
- Accept the fact that there are certain situations in which you won't win no matter what. If discouragement doesn't get the best of you, you'll remember that you'll have another chance again. At the end of the day, some decisions are made solely on chemistry. Life is not logical nor fair. I remember a company president who remarked he was not going to hire a particular marketing person because the man's wife wasn't classy enough!
- Surprise them. Come back later with something like, "I know this didn't work out. You made a business decision and I respect that. If there is some

way I can help in a future situation, feel free to call me."

Regardless of good intent, you'll make mistakes. Failures won't kill you. Pick up and start over.

And keeping with the habit of looking at things with a different perspective, let me point out about job hunting at the six-figure level:

- No best friend will be completely unhappy about your failure.
- It isn't a disgrace to be searching, just an inconvenience.
- Pain, temporary lack of income, disgrace, and disappointment are good—they restore your abilities and make you strong.
- The goal you're striving for is pretty stiff; it's a major financial achievement. It will take some work, but you are up to it.

Define what you're good at, what you want to do, and what is needed by a company that has the money to pay you six figures.

As I mentioned before, the job function you choose should have the market potential of paying $100K-plus. If it doesn't (as in jobs like nurse, teacher, cop, secretary), no matter how good you are, you're not likely to make your financial objective. That doesn't mean you won't be perfectly happy and invaluable to society. And that doesn't mean you can't change job functions to a traditionally higher-paying job as you move along in your career.

Most Americans switch *careers* three times in a lifetime. Here's a sample of the average number of years spent in certain careers according to the U.S. Department of Labor:

Accountants	8 years
Administrators, managers, supervisors	9
Aerospace engineers	10
Airplane pilots	14
Authors	6
Bank tellers	4
Barbers	25
Billing clerks	6
Bookkeepers and auditing clerks	7
Carpenters	8
Chemical engineers	9
Child-care workers	3
Civil engineers	13
Clergy	16
Data equipment repairers	7
Doctors, dentists, veterinarians	12
Drafters and mechanical drawers	8
Economists	5
Editors and reporters	6
Electrical and electronic technicians	7
Electricians	11
Financial managers	8
Financial service sales	5
Firefighters	10
Garage and service station workers	3

Guards	3
Health record technicians	3
Heat and air-conditioning mechanics	8
Hotel clerks	3
Industrial engineers	9
Industrial truck and tractor operators	7
Insurance adjusters and investigators	5
Lawyers	10
Librarians	9
Licensed practical nurses	10
Mail carriers	7
Musicians and composers	8
Office clerks	4
Painters, construction and maintenance	6
Personnel clerks	5
Personnel trainers	5
Pharmacists	12
Photographers	8
Physical therapists	5
Police officers, sheriffs, bailiffs	10
Production coordinators	6
Psychologists	8
Real estate sales	6
Sales representatives	9
Secretaries	8
Social workers	8
Taxi drivers	4
Teachers, elementary to high school	12
Water and sewage plant operators	8

If you are making a radical shift to get into or move around at the $100K level, talk to people already in the job functions you've targeted. Ask them two basic questions:

- What's the best part of this work?
- What's the worst part?

(Again, since conversations take time to both set up and have, it's best to be doing this while still employed—long before you need to.)

Too often people think of conversations like I just recommended as job-hunting-related. They aren't. They are keeping a dialogue going with people outside of your own specific world—the same type of dialogue necessary with your boss regarding your job performance and progress. The only difference is this kind of conversation is popularly labeled networking.

At the $100K level, the absolutely most efficient way to get a new job is through your contacts—who you know, and what they know about you.

The basis of civilization is communication with people. Perseverance in personal contact is critical.

The basis of good communication is establishing, maintaining, and reviving contact with people when you *don't* need something from them. Then if you do, you'll be more likely to get a natural, easy, comfortable, helpful reception.

Think about someone you know: the one who telephones occasionally to say hello, shares a tidbit about something of interest to you, mentions that your name came up in a conversation, tells you about a new book on fly fishing (a sport he knows you relish), inquires how your job is going, seeks your opinion on a venture of his. If that casual business friendship is fostered over a period of time, it's only natural for that person to contact you when he is looking for a new job. In fact, you might even be a little miffed if he doesn't ask for your help and suggestions. (Your contacts will feel the same way about you if you treat them that way.)

People always want to be associated with winners. If you are good at what you do, people will proudly and eagerly do all they can to help. They are realistic, knowing you'll likely do the same for them when they ask.

Your day does not need to be consumed with networking minutiae. It only requires consistent periodic effort to stay in touch with people you like, respect, and learn from. Every now and then, out of the blue, send an article of potential interest to them with your business card attached. Even if they already have the article, you'll stay in their mind in an unobtrusive way. Remember, it's easier to keep a good contact than to make a new one.

Bear in mind my suggestion that potential employers need to hear of you four times before you approach them for a job. The same rule of thumb can be applied in general interpersonal communication. Initiate contact with people four times before you need them.

The more people you stay in contact with—outside of day-to-day co-workers—the more people who'll *know* you. People hire people they know, or a person someone they *know,* knows. According to Labor Department statistics, seven out of ten job hunters find jobs through networking with friends, relatives, and acquaintances.

Okay, so you have a limited number of friends and relatives (including in-laws, brothers and sisters, half-brothers and -sisters, cousins, aunts, uncles), but your acquaintances are almost unlimited: neighbors, ex-neighbors, doctor, lawyer, tax preparer, printer, home builder, real estate agent, teachers, minister, childrens' friends' parents, church friends, banker, postman, retailers, repairman, city officials, politicians, classmates, barber, beautician, cleaner, tailor, ex–co-workers, suppliers, delivery people, customers, competitors, health or social clubs, and charitable organization members—just to jog your memory.

Not every one of them will necessarily get the notice of the new book on fly fishing—but some might! Each one of them can get the two extra seconds of paying attention to detail that were mentioned earlier—so you remember them, so they remember you.

Statistics show that 55 percent of people in the United States will be in a different job a year from now. Think of the wealth of information your contacts have on their old company, organizations they researched and interviewed with, and the company they finally joined.

I mentioned the importance of researching good companies. The absolute best way to find out about an organization is from people who might know about it: employees, ex-employees, customers, competitors, vendors, suppliers, business reporters, chamber of commerce. With a little luck someone in your circle of contacts knows the right person to talk to.

If an individual you communicate with knows and likes you and your track record, she might tell you about specific job openings, introduce you to a recruiter friend of hers, set up an appointment with someone who makes the hiring decision in a company, provide inside information on the needs, concerns, or personality of a key boss, recommend your hiring, or be an advocate once the interview is over by talking to the boss and reiterating support for you.

A senior executive who always hires people at the six-figure level says, "I'll always take a referral. I treat candidates based on how I got their name."

Enough has been written about networking that you *know* its value; the question is whether you will put it into practice as a daily part of your life. There is only an upside to doing it—absolutely no downside. At the $100K level, it is another one of those things absolutely critical for success.

Just like you need to quantify your worth to your employer, you need to quantify your worth to a *prospective* employer on paper.

Ideally you get in the door of a prospective company through a qualified referral. But let's say you are on your own. Your marketing tools must communicate, in a limited amount of space, your competence and experience.

At the six-figure jobs you are competing for, your marketing tools will likely include an approach letter, a résumé and cover letter, supplemental accomplishment case write-ups, and personalized note cards for follow-up. Any *one* of these tools can be all that is necessary for successfully securing a job. More than likely, though, you'll use more than one, so you might as well have them prepared.

An approach letter is written dialogue to test potential mutual interest. It's used to follow-up a referral someone gave to you, touch base with a good contact, follow-up on an article in the paper, or to seek general information. An approach letter can stand alone or be attached to a résumé.

Some brief samples:

> Dear ________,
>
> I was quite interested in the recent article in the *Post* regarding the ________.
>
> Although I'm currently involved in _______, I've found interaction with other people who have _______ and would like to offer my assistance.
>
> One approach that could be effective _______ [as you offer an idea].
>
> Feel free to contact me to discuss this application ________.
>
> Regards,

> Dear ________,
>
> After twenty years with XYZ, I'm looking for a _______ position, in which I can help expand

_________, enhance _________, and develop _________.

I've earned my stripes the old-fashioned way . . . I've worked for them (among some darn good companies, incidentally).

I'm not the fast-talking, promise-them-anything, slap-them-on-the-back type. My style is calm, cool, persuasive.

My strength is _________. I can wear several hats, such as _________.

I am certain you are quite busy, but a half hour at your office or perhaps a luncheon meeting could be quite worthwhile for both of us.

I'll be calling you soon.

P.S. I am usually at home after 7 P.M. weekdays.

Dear _________,

I wanted to update you on my situation at _________.

The recent acquisition resulted in _________.

There is no pressure for me to find immediate employment. I prefer to find the right situation _________.

The most interesting job positions would be _________.

Naturally, I value your opinion and any thoughts you might have _________.

Regards,

Dear _________,

If you are like other key executives in the

__________ industry, you are confronted with the problems of __________.

As a regional manager for a __________, I found that __________. When you read my résumé, you will see that I:

- Took over a __________, negotiated a ______, increased sales __________, and changed the bottom line from red to black
- Reopened __________
- Set new performance standards __________

Although I haven't met you personally, Mr. ______, I'm aware of your reputation at __________. Perhaps you are aware of firms that would consider the right man if he came along. I'd appreciate your opinion. In a few days, I'll be contacting you. Or, in the meantime, I can be reached in the evening at __________.

Sincerely,

The letter should be succinct and clear, yet interesting as well. The recipients are busy people who undoubtedly receive a lot of correspondence each week. Your letter needs to be written like you have made an effort to study their business in some detail. A line such as "I note with interest in the *Wall Street Journal* . . ." isn't what I mean. A statement like "Since ____ is happening in your company, you need me" is more effective.

Then provide a to-the-point summary of results that

you've accomplished that would interest the potential employer and that relate to what you know about the company. It would be unreasonable to tell people how to run their company. You are practically a total stranger to their organization and it would appear arrogant and foolish to try to shape them up. Rather, demonstrate enthusiasm, courage, and motivation by putting forth the effort to stand out from the rest by revealing your knowledge of your potential employer's company.

Like a letter, your résumé should be interesting, accurate, tailored to the employer, and clear. The reason for this conciseness? Despite the fact that your résumé tells the reader so much—what you're looking for, what you have to offer, jobs you've had, and education—he or she will likely spend only ten seconds reading it!

A Note About Job Hunting Courage

I've had clients and friends review the letters I've just given as examples, and some have said, "It would take some courage to write a letter like that to someone I don't know."

My response is, "Ha! That's nothing! Those sentences on a sheet of paper are milquetoast compared to what you have to do in an actual job situation if you're going for the brass ring!"

You probably wouldn't even be reading this book if you didn't have the intestinal fortitude required to go after a big-paying job. But if you are still on the fence a little, jump off. Jump into this scary new territory. If you don't, you won't make the big bucks.

Think about the situation you are in: There are one hundred people applying for the same job as you. You all have comparable degrees, references, work experience, and IQ level. What will set you apart? Your attitude and willingness to do what others don't. That means being *different* to stand out. *Important distinction: Different does not mean weird.*

Let me tell you about two different situations recently in which I used courage. I wasn't job hunting per se because I'm self-employed. But getting a new assignment isn't dissimilar from getting a new job—you just have to do it more frequently. So you could say I job hunt all of the time, and that starts with contacts.

The first situation: I was at a conference in southern California where the CEO of Pepsi-Cola was speaking. I had been a consultant to the company for many years but had not met the new CEO. He finished his remarks and sat down. He was in the middle of the room and several steps away from the door. After a while he got up to leave. Since I had positioned myself near the door, I was able to step out first, long before he got there. Once outside, I waited in the hallway for thirty or forty seconds, anticipating he would also step out. When he did, I was right there.

I went up to him and introduced myself as a consultant working with his company and complimented him on some points in his speech I thought particularly valuable. Then I put my hand on his shoulder and kiddingly said, "You're not nearly as scary as some people make you out to be."

He laughed. Then he asked, "Your name was what? And who have you worked for at the company?" Because of the courage to be personable and to use humor, I set myself apart, in his mind, from the other hundred people who might have had the opportunity to meet him in the hallway. He wanted to remember my name.

A second situation: I was at the Ritz Carlton in Naples, Florida. The hotel is located on one of the most beautiful beaches in the country. I was riding up in the elevator with a man who had just checked in. As he inserted his key in the elevator to reach the concierge floor, I kidded him: "They save those rooms for very important people."

He laughed and said, "Well, they might have made a mistake in this case."

Then I said to him, "You look familiar. Should I know you?"

He responded, "I'm Joe Hardiman, CEO of NASDAQ. I'm speaking at the NIRI [National Investor Relations Institute] conference tomorrow."

"I'm Debra Benton. I'm also speaking at the conference," I answered. By this time we had reached our floor and were parting ways.

I got into my hotel room and thought, *What a gorgeous beach. It'd make for a nice walk. I'll ask Mr. Hardiman if he'd like to go with me.* So I called the hotel operator and had her connect me to his room. "Mr. Hardiman, this is Debra Benton, the woman you met in the elevator. It's a beautiful day. Would you have time to go for a walk?"

He answered, "Okay. I'll meet you in the lobby in fifteen minutes."

We met, walked on the beach, had a delightful conversation about our respective work, families, interests—our alls! He had an early evening meeting with some of his staff, so we returned to the lobby and shook hands good-bye.

The next morning when he addressed the thousand-person audience, the first words out of his mouth were a plug for my seminar, to be held the next day!

Both of those situations took courage. Because of my willingness to do what others don't do, I have two good new acquaintances.

You can (and must) be different and better, in person as well as on paper. Having worked with many $100K Club member résumés, I recommend the following format to both stand out from the crowd and convey your information clearly:

- Job objective
- Summary of experience
- Accomplishments

- Work experience
- Education
- Personal information

The *job objective* describes in a sentence or two the job you'd like to do. With computers you can easily tailor every résumé to fit the situation you're going for. For example, if you're writing a résumé for an entrepreneur who has a start-up company providing products in a four-state area, you wouldn't want to state "want to work for multidivision international company" in your job objective. You might put, instead, "want to work in an entrepreneurial start-up organization with vast growth potential."

If you don't clearly state where you want to go, the employer won't guess accurately and you'll likely not get what you want. You can be honest but flexible in your job objective. Under the right circumstances an entrepreneurial situation could interest you, as well as an international job. Be focused yet flexible.

The *summary of experience* should be in a "snapshot" format. Research shows a typical reader spends ten seconds on average with your résumé. Since the person has already used three seconds on your name and job objective, you only have seven seconds to hold her attention and get her to read on. You started out in two sentences stating where you want to go; now you're providing a summary of where you've been.

For example:

Summary of Experience

- Have supervised up to 40 people
- Speak three languages
- Managed budgets of $1.5 to $3 million
- Responsible for research and development of two new products
- Worked in six countries
- Have master's in finance and marketing

If the reader has remained interested this far, she may want more detail. Provide that in brief case descriptions of accomplishments.

Accomplishments are mini-case stories of successes. They are organized by stating the situation, relating your contribution, and giving the result.

The accomplishment cases you include in any specific résumé should be relevant to the person you are writing to. It's like the job objective—tailored to the reader. If you've networked into this potential employer, you likely know more about her than others, and that helps you decide which success stories to include.

You will have many more accomplishment cases than you'll have room for in your résumé, so keep additional ones for follow-up. Say you sent a résumé and cover letter, and had an interview that was cut short by some emergency on the interviewer's part. You can send a thank-you note for her time and interest and suggest, "Had we had more time to talk, we would likely have discussed __________. I'm enclosing a few additional examples of my contributions to give you a more complete picture of what I can bring to your company."

An example of an accomplishment might read:

> Reduced operating expenses by ten million dollars in an eighty-million-dollar organization while the bottom line quadrupled. Featured on the front page of the *Wall Street Journal* for refashioning one of the most expensive organizations to one of the most efficient and effective in the United States. Received Organizational Innovators Award from the Industry Forum.

Three to four of these cases are all you'll have room for in the résumé. The job objective, summary of experience, and accomplishments complete the first page of the résumé.

Some people contend a résumé should be one page only. I don't care if it is five pages or one—if it is boring, it's too long. But if you've experienced significant successes (and at the $100K level, you have), you need a certain amount of space to communicate them and that's generally going to take nearly two full pages—maybe three.

Work experience starts the second page. This section is a chronological history giving:

- Company name
- Location

- Month and year of employment
- A one-sentence job description

An entry might read:

XYZ Corporation, New York,
Vice President 12/92–10/97
Marketing responsibilities for eastern region in X product line.

If you've had a thirty-five-year career, go back in detail for the last fifteen or twenty years. Then do a summary paragraph of the first fifteen years.

The next part of the résumé is *education,* including continuing education. List college, degree(s), dates. The longer you've been out of the traditional education track, the more important it is to list significant continuing education via seminars, workshops, or special consulting.

Next, include some *personal information.* (Remember your alls.) You need to show some human aspects of yourself, a little personality, some interests outside of the office. The employer is hiring a person, not a machine. Don't be leery of listing marital status, age, hobbies, personal interests—regardless of what you've read elsewhere.

John Moore, president of Electro-Test, told me, "Sometimes I skip right over experience and degrees and look for hobbies and outside interests—the balance in the person's life. If they have nothing outside of business that they are involved in, that scares me. If two candidates were comparable, and everything equal, but one was active in Soroptimists, for example, that's who I'd hire. I've found people with outside interests have a higher energy level."

In my youth, fresh out of college I included "sailing and autocrossing" (racing cars against a clock) as hobbies on my résumé. My first employer assigned executive mentors to new hires. The executives could pick who they wanted to work with. The individual who picked me also sailed and autocrossed. Later he told me it was hard to distinguish one new college graduate from another, so the personal section got the attention. (It may not have hurt that I also listed "former Miss Colorado Teen-ager." Hey, you have to use what you have!)

A personal data entry might read:

> Happily married. Willing to travel and relocate. Active running 10K road races and collecting antique clocks.

Some people who hire $100K-plus people tell me they could care less about the personal section. Others say it's the first thing they read. That is a typical reaction to all parts of a résumé: Each individual will have preferences. The format I've recommended reflects the interests of most of the top people, most of the time.

A résumé should be a current, interesting-to-read record of your professional life. It is not something you whip up when you need a job. It is an ongoing tool you update every six months.

If you don't keep it current, you forget the details of what you've accomplished. And if you can't remember or communicate your accomplishments clearly, I can assure you, no one else will know or care.

In addition to the résumé, maintain a complete and current file on yourself that includes:

- Articles, editorials, and letters to the editor that you've written
- Clippings where you have been quoted or mentioned
- Media interviews or speeches you've given
- Copies of awards or other recognitions

Obviously, if this file is completely empty, start working on getting significant pieces into it. Search firms maintain data banks of potential job candidates. Good firms pride themselves on their research files. Their research comes from tracking who's who and who's doing what as reported in business journals.

This file has the information in it that might have been where prospective employers, headhunters, and centers of influence have heard of you one or more of the four times necessary.

The time to work on a résumé is when you do not need one, so you are more objective (less emotional) about yourself. But remember, a résumé does not get you a job. Your creativity, resourcefulness, tenacity, and ability (and even agility) get you the job.

One man I know wanted to work for the governor of Colorado. He sent letters, résumés, and made telephone calls. No interest. He received only perfunctory responses. Then he started a planned letter-to-the-editor writing campaign to the *Denver Post* and *Rocky Mountain News*—two publications the governor and his staff paid attention to. The letters were designed to address solutions to problems while establishing the writer's expertise on the subject—one particular subject of keen interest to the governor. One of the politician's staff members read the letters, contacted the writer, and asked if he'd consider discussing those issues with the governor personally. The résumé did not get him an entrée, his resourcefulness did. He ended up being hired for the governor's staff.

You have to initiate being discovered: first by doing good work and more than required, and then by making sure the right people know it.

The objective of a résumé, like a job interview, is for the hiring organization to:

- Understand your accomplishments
- Identify capabilities and strengths as needed by the company
- Determine potential of fitting in
- Verify claims

The personalized note cards I mentioned earlier are to follow up every conversation you have with everyone and anyone. The card size, approximately 4 x 7-1/2 inches, with matching envelope (available through

Crane & Company in Dalton, Massachusetts), allows for a two- to three-sentence, handwritten message. It's the kind of message CEOs send back and forth to each other. I maintain a collection of samples in my files in which six- and seven-figure people write back and forth to each other with letters that say no more than "Thanks" or "Great job, glad to see you in print" or "Keep me posted on the progress and outcome" or simply "Yes" to some question that was posed.

I tested this theory when I wrote my first book, *Lions Don't Need to Roar.* I wrote to two hundred company presidents to request an interview for my book. The letter was neatly typed on standard-sized typewriter paper. It included four paragraphs explaining my purpose, request, and follow-up. I received zero response.

So I thought about presidents and CEOs and other top people who write to each other and I followed their example. I used the 4 x 7-1/2 cards with only my name embossed on it. I hand wrote a two-sentence letter, "You'd be a good person to interview for my book on traits at the top. Could I have thirty minutes of your time in April? Sincerely, Debra Benton," and I included my phone number.

That handwritten note went out to two hundred different company heads. Twenty-five percent responded within two weeks. More followed.

One of these Crane cards gets sent out of my office, in my own handwriting, *daily.*

They've gone:

- To people I've read about in the newspaper or magazine or have seen on television. Sometimes I know the people, sometimes I want to get to know them, but first I always congratulate them personally in writing
- To the children of clients about the special parent they have, or about an achievement of their own that their parents told me about
- To people I know who have been ill and appreciate my get-well wishes
- To detractors, with the sentiment, "I learn something from everyone . . . even you"
- To politicians regarding legislation
- To friends who got new jobs
- To acquaintances about a speech I heard that might interest them, and I insert the speech in with the card

The list is endless.

If I go on vacation and miss sending the daily card, I take a half hour out of my return day and do five at one time.

The point is, it's a constant activity.

Eight out of ten times I don't hear from the person (a fact that always surprises me). But two of the ten times something unexpected, but welcome, happens.

That unexpected—but welcome—something is what I want you to experience in your job hunt and career. It makes it a whole lot more fun!

D. A. BENTON

JOB INTERVIEWING FOR SIX-FIGURE JOBS

The job interview should be the easiest part of a job search for *my* readers because you are so skilled at keeping dialogue going on your job. A job interview is no different from any other conversation, except the focus is on your capabilities as they fit a potential employers' needs.

The primary success traits (assuming competence in the job) looked for at this level are:

- *People orientation.* Do you value others equally as yourself? Do you give more than you take? Do you take the initiative? Do you talk about others and their interests instead of just your own?
- *Good judgment.* Do you have a value system that adds to life experiences? Do they add to the corporate culture's values?
- *Curiosity.* Since that's the basis for innovation and ingenuity, are you interested in how things are and how they can be changed? Do you see change as part of being or as something to fear?
- *Results orientation.* Do you push the process toward results or toward making yourself a hero? Can you sustain through the ups and downs. What lives on after you're gone?

That's what employers want to see, and that's where attitude, attention to detail, and fearlessness are required. If you've done a good job writing up your accomplishments for the résumé, you have the stories to use in the interview to provide evidence of your claims.

An interview, like a conversation, is a two-way street regarding questions, answers, observations, opinions, and the rest of effective communication. Do not make the mistake of going there to impress; go there to learn. Your potential employer is screening you as you are screening him.

No matter how prepared you are going in, you'll never know quite what your potential employer is looking for. So ask. He is going to ask you plenty of questions; you can ask him just as many. Remember Mark Wheless from Pepsi-Cola, and his advice: You are there to contribute. That includes a job interview.

Keep in mind, most people are as nervous being the interviewer as you are being the interviewee. They are searching for the best possible person to fit into their company; they don't want to mess up their chance of getting the best. If you are interviewing at the $100K level, they know you must be good, and good people have lots of options. They don't want to lose you, if they want you—so they are as anxious as you are about being impressive.

Job interviewing is an imprecise science for both the interviewee and the interviewer.

Linn Leeburg of Public Service Company of Colorado told me, "We go through an incredibly elaborate assessment of people and sometimes I think if we walked out the door and grabbed the first person to come along, we'd do just as well."

The interviewer may ask myriad questions ranging from banal to brilliant. In a moment I'm going to list a number of actual questions used at six-figure-income-level interviews. When you are actively job hunting, I'd suggest you let your spouse or significant other ask each one of these aloud and that you answer aloud. It is best to record this role-playing and listen to it on the car radio as you drive to and from job interviews.

Just as you prepare to be interviewed, interviewers prepare to interview. They are taught:

- Don't get to the point that you are desperate to take someone. If you wait until you are overwhelmed before you start looking for help, it's too late and the candidate will likely be hired out of desperation.
- Think about what you are truly trying to achieve by hiring this person. What justifies the paycheck?
- Prepare a list of questions in advance and ask the same questions of everybody to get comparable information. Don't wing it or let a charismatic interviewee derail you.
- Structure the questions to force the candidate to explain, not just report or claim. In other words, the résumé likely reported a lot of positive information; the interview should substantiate the information and discover the "so what" about it.
- Refrain from doing too much talking. A smart job

hunter will be asking you lots of questions, but don't let him or her control the conversation.

- Resist the urge to hire someone on the spot either out of desperation or fear of losing a "good one." Have more people spend more time to get a complete size-up. Specifically, include in the interviews people who would be potential co-workers.

Since you know your potential employer is planning her questions, I'll start with some traditional ones, then move into the more creative ones.

- Tell me about yourself.
- Why are you interested in joining our company?
- What do you see yourself doing five years from now?
- Who else have you interviewed with?
- What sort of money are you looking for?
- What are your strengths and weaknesses?
- Why do you feel you're qualified for this job?
- Why did you leave XYZ company?
- I'm a bit worried about your experience in __________.
- What do you like to do in your spare time?
- Why do you want to change careers?
- Ever have a disagreement with a boss? Why? Why not? What did you do about it?
- Have you ever been fired?
- If hired, how long would it take for you to make significant contributions to our company?
- How would you describe your management style?

Now some of the more creative questions:

- What do you expect from a boss?
- How do you affect people?
- If there was something you could change about yourself, what would it be and why?
- If I asked you to produce your W-2 from last year, what would it say?
- How many hours are in your workday?
- What makes you happy? Unhappy?
- Talk about your failures. Tell me more.
- Give me a verbal autobiography.
- What should I know about you that we haven't already discussed?
- Tell me about your best friend in high school. What would they say about you?
- Tell me about the most entrepreneurial thing you've ever done.
- Everyone has detractors, what do yours say about you?
- Pick a workday last week and tell me about the day. Start with when you woke up, and tell me hour by hour what you did until you went to bed again. Now pick a day last weekend and do the same thing.
- When you had recent performance appraisals, what did they say was your best attribute? What did they say they wanted you to work on?

You can see that the direction an interviewer takes can vary tremendously.

What's the best way to handle questions in general? Answer with a question, or a story, or both.

For example, when they say "Tell me about yourself," answer: "I'd be happy to tell you about myself. Are you more interested in my professional experience, educational background, or what I do in my free time?"

By asking a question you clarify their interests, buy yourself time to think of the answer to give, and set yourself apart from others who blurt out their life story.

Interviewers will likely say "Your work experience," but sometimes they pick other areas, and that tells you something about them.

Say they've asked about your work experience. Give them the answer in a succinct, chronological format. When you've finished the explanation, ask one of the following questions to clarify and verify where you are:

- Did that answer your question?
- Would you like to know more detail?
- How does that background fit in with your requirements?

In a matter of minutes you've set yourself apart from your competitors, while learning (and earning) a valuable nugget for yourself.

Another question interviewers like: "What are your strengths and weaknesses?"

Most people answer with a version of "I'm good with people, I have a strong technical competence, and I have lots of enthusiasm for my work. My weakness is never having enough time to get everything completed."

That's a typical, boring answer.

When you answer your strengths first and weaknesses last (like they asked), you end the conversation on a negative point. Start by saying, "Let me talk about weaknesses first and get them out of the way; then I'll talk about my strengths." (Again, you've set yourself apart in a subtle way.)

When you give a weakness, make it a positive weakness like "I have very little patience for people who don't carry out what they commit to." You can induce a little levity into the conversation with "And another weakness is chocolate."

When you start listing your strengths, attribute your self-evaluation to someone else: "My boss at XYZ company would say I'm good with people. My subordinates would tell you I have great enthusiasm for my work." (Obviously your boss and subordinates must be willing to say that, because they will likely be asked when it comes time to check references.)

When describing strengths, accomplishments, or capabilities, it's best to tell a supporting story. Describe what you did in a successful situation and what resulted. People believe and enjoy stories rather than claims and platitudes.

Regarding the former boss saying you are good with people, you could add: "When I joined XYZ, I inherited a team that was not getting along. So I met privately with each member over a couple of weeks and learned what their goals and frustrations were. Then I sorted out the lists of information gathered and found a strong common theme that went through every one of the conversations. I brought them together and reported on my findings. The way I expressed their feedback brought some chuckles, but they all agreed there was considerable consensus among them. Since that meeting they've worked as an extremely cohesive team, even winning a company-wide award."

Again, the same case stories you developed for the résumé are used to better illustrate and answer questions in the interview.

Another common question: "What do you want to be doing five years from now?" This is a broad, general question needing to be clarified.

You can say, "Five years from now I have lots of goals. Are you interested in where I'd like to be in this company, or what I want to have accomplished in continuing education, or what I'd like to be doing personally?"

Typically they'll say, "Where you want to be in your career." So tell them, then ask, "If I do good work, is that going to be possible?"

You see how you're engaging in a conversation similar to one you would have with a friend you feel comfortable with?

Two important things to remember in the interview: First, ask questions at the beginning, in the middle, and at the end. Don't wait until they ask, "Any questions?" Second, bring up the difficult-to-answer questions first, before they do.

If they try to fluster you with something like "What would last year's W-2 show as income exactly?" you have missed an opportunity to handle the uncomfortable money issue on your own initiative.

Instead, before they bring up money, do it yourself. "Money is not my main motivation, but I am curious, what is the pay range for this position?" If their answer is at the level or more than you expected, say, "That's within the range I'm looking for." If it was below what you expected, ask, "Under what circumstances can that be increased? What would one have to do to get to _________ level—which is what I'm looking for." (It's better to know now than be surprised later.)

Or, say, you were fired from your last job. Before they ask about it (a fact they will likely discover while checking references), you might say something earlier: "Would you be interested in the circumstances surrounding my departure from XYZ?"

If they say yes, give an honest, brief explanation without pointing fingers. Do not go on and on defensively, nor do you need to be confessional or emotional.

It's better to bring up bad news yourself and handle it when and *how* you want to.

A rule of thumb for asking questions: Anything they've asked you, you can ask them. For example, you can ask the interviewer, "Tell me about yourself . . . where do you want to be five years from now . . . what are the company's strengths and weaknesses?"

Other questions could (and should) be:

- What kind of person do you want for this position?
- What's important about the person you hire?
- How many people have held this position in the last two years?
- Would you describe a typical workday and the things I'd be doing?
- How does this job contribute to the company?
- Is this department a profit center for the company?
- Are sales up or down over the last year?
- Where can someone in this job be promoted to?
- How will success be measured in this position?
- How long do you think it will take until you make a decision?

Make sure people answer your questions, just like you answer theirs. If they give a vague, general response, ask, "Can you give me an example?"

Concentrate more on listening and grasping what they're saying than on thinking ahead to what you are going to say next. Keep in mind at all times that you are trying to minimize their concerns about things like:

- Is he lazy?
- Does she have common sense?
- Does he have fire in the belly?
- Is she qualified?
- Is he lying?
- Will she fit in?
- Will he embarrass me?

While the interviewer is trying to find that out about you, you are trying to find out:

- Is the company worth joining?
- Do they have good products or services?
- Do they have workable plans for the future?
- Will I have a qualified, competent boss?
- Will they support my growth and development?
- Will they reward my efforts?
- Will I be proud to work for them?
- Can I make $100K and more?

When you get home after the interview, debrief yourself on what you learned and what you still need to find out. Don't rely on memory. Write it down. Finally, ask yourself: Did people laugh during your interview, did people seem to like each other, was there an air of secrecy or openness, was anyone working late?

EXECUTIVE RECRUITERS

The best way to job hunt is by doing exemplary work on the job. It will be noticed inside and outside of the company. People know who is doing the good work.

But sometimes outside recruiters enter the picture. There are two types of headhunters: retainer and contingency. At the six-figure level you want to deal with retainer firms. Senior-level jobs are more likely filled by retainer search firms. *Retainer* means the firm gets their 33 percent fee, plus expenses, at the start of the search—regardless of whether they complete the search or not. A contingency firm only gets paid after (and if) they fill the position; often their contacts are no better than yours.

Retainer firms often complete their searches successfully. They have to perform, one, because they've been paid, and, two, for their professional reputation. Still, occasionally a contingency firm will have an assignment for a $100K job. You want to find out which type of firm you're dealing with at the beginning of any conversations.

Either type of recruiter lives by his sources. Become one and you'll be recruited in the future.

If you aren't actively job hunting yourself, when a headhunter calls you about a job—unless it is the *dream* job of your life—offer to help the recruiter find qualified candidates. Say something like, "I'm doing well here . . . I'm not really interested in another position. Some of the things I'm working on hold lots of promise. Based on what you've told me about the job, I'd suggest you talk to __________."

Only if you have a good network of people going will you know someone exceptional to suggest—someone deliverable to the client. Obviously you don't want to recommend some loser.

Remember dating in high school? The more someone turned you down, the more attractive he or she became?

The same thing happens to a recruiter. After a couple of years of a relationship with a sharp recruiter in which you continually (and helpfully) brush offers aside, you will be so attractive to her you can write your own ticket to a dream job.

A female vice president I talked to who handles recruiters this way told me, "I had three calls on my voice mail today from recruiters because of the network relationship I've developed with them." Don't you think that when she gets interested in looking for a job, they will return her phone call?

Another good reason for recruiter relationships is they are a good source of market value as it relates to: position, responsibility, head count, revenue, and salary range. They have the most current information on what your market value is.

CONCLUSION

If you are guilty of any of the following, put a check beside it:

☐ Procrastination
☐ Lack of organization
☐ Lack of specific goal

- ☐ Low level of drive
- ☐ Self-criticism
- ☐ Low self-confidence
- ☐ Perfectionism
- ☐ Fear of looking foolish
- ☐ Fear of failure
- ☐ Blaming other people
- ☐ Fear of meeting new people
- ☐ Fear of rejection
- ☐ Continual paper shuffling
- ☐ Negative attitude
- ☐ Difficulty in making decisions
- ☐ Loss of self-esteem
- ☐ Poor co-worker relationships

For every check on this list, add a month of job search time to the typical length of one month for every ten thousand dollars of income.

At the $100K level, your best bet may be to create a job—either inside a company or by creating your own entrepreneurial venture. If so, the next chapter is for you.

"It is not enough to chart a course; you must plan an attack. Find yourself a mentor and treat him or her like your own personal board of directors. Like any executive, set goals and prepare and deliver regular reports to your mentors. Share your ideas, plan, and learn to strategize. The most important step is to believe you can make it!"

—STEVE SEKIGUCHI,
Wind River Systems, Inc.

"Obtain an undergraduate degree in liberal arts. Take language courses and a couple of introductory accounting courses. Make certain that you're computer-literate. Pursue an MBA (perhaps after working a couple of years). Take international business courses. After college, join a consulting firm. If that's not possible, change jobs (not necessarily companies) every couple of years until you're around thirty. The goal is to create a diversity of experiences that provide several options to advance your career."

—RICHARD JACOBS,
CFO

"Know your subject backward and forward. Nonsubstantive types may get ahead, but you don't want to be one of them. Ultimately they're found out.

"Prosper from every job. What doesn't kill you, improves you. Don't waste a learning experience loathing your job. You won't learn and you'll make yourself and everyone else miserable.

"Watch others. What makes them successful? Could you do what they do? Would you want to be where they are? Plan your future based on your strengths and what you've learned in the past.

"Do the right thing. Stand on principle. Honor your moral code. Going along to get along ultimately gets you. No one trusts a moral coward."

—William Perry Pendley,
CEO, Western States
Employment Council

CHAPTER 6

How to Earn $100K at Home or on Your Own

On a farm in upstate New York, a marine attorney who became an international fish quality assurance checker types a fax into his computer. While he sleeps, the fax goes to customers on fishing trawlers all around the world. His wife faxes him her schedule from a speaking assignment in San Francisco. She is a self-employed political analyst. Included in her transmission is the grocery list she wants him to pick up on his way into town to ship a package to Florida. Between the two of them, they earn $250K a year out of their home, on their own.

Like the attorney and his wife, you have a unique set of personal and professional experiences, training, and abilities that can put you into your own successful business.

Others who have turned their abilities and interests into successful businesses:

- From a houseboat in Vancouver harbor, a seventy-five-year-old man, fascinated with the unknown, calls himself a futurist. He earns $450K through writing newspaper columns, speeches, CD-ROM books, and radio sound bites about the future.
- A former funeral director and his wife clean up crime scenes where homicides, suicides, and accidents cause grisly messes. By their third year of operation, sales were over a million dollars.
- A former health food newsletter editor turned from health food trade show displayer to purchaser of trade shows, to food exporter, to becoming the biggest importer of plywood from Russia to the United States—and works from his Colorado home.
- A computer company replacement-component shipper fulfilled an overload of customer service parts out of his garage on overtime. He was so efficient in satisfying customers that the company turned all replacement-order fulfillment over to him. When customers call the computer company department, the phone rings in the new business owner's garage "fulfillment center."
- A retired high school teacher and counselor loved classical music. She held concerts in her home, recording musician friends with her own semiprofessional recording equipment. Contracting the record pressing to big producers and using her garage as a warehouse in 1976, her enterprise grew to a $4 million business with twenty-eight employees by 1995.

- The leading breeder of designer snakes—such as patterned albino pythons—houses them in his home (to his wife's dismay). He gets $1,500 a snake versus the $100 that common snake breeders get.
- An ex–executive recruiter from Chicago left the stress-filled world to follow her interests. Now, in Maine, she makes custom jigsaw puzzles. In the last few years she has sold four thousand puzzles at $3,500 a piece.
- A biscotti (twice-baked cookie) baker began testing recipes in the kitchen of her two-family home. She started by clearing only $40 a week in 1981. Sales in 1996 will be $9 million. Her husband, daughter, father, and mother all work in the business.

Although these businesses are a bit more unusual than most, there is a plethora of at-home six-figure income earners doing the more typical work of consultants, accountants, manufacturers' representatives, temporary secretarial services, television repairmen, plumbers, and artists.

There are also attorneys, writers, engineers, public relations people, salespeople, graphic designers, independent insurance agents, financial planners, real estate agents, editors, photographers, computer experts, composers, and carpenters.

An AT&T survey showed the breakdown of people working on their own: 51 percent of those are service firms, 17 percent in sales, 15 percent in technical and administrative support, 11 percent in repair services, and 5 percent or so in the arts.

Fact is, many of those businesses will fail. *Fail* to become a million-dollar or billion-dollar operation. But many will also *succeed* in providing the founder with a comfortable six-figure income.

On the other hand, you might succeed beyond your most unrealistic dreams. *Forbes* magazine wrote, "Annually, we publish a directory showing how much chief executives earn in major corporations. Every fall *Forbes* compiles a list of the 400 richest Americans. Did you ever wonder why there is so little overlap between the two categories, CEOs and superrich? Among the 400 wealthiest people in the U.S. only a small fraction ever served as chief executives of major corporations. Almost none were hired hands, career executives running companies funded by others. Earning a salary, even a fat salary, is not the road to riches."

IS WORKING ON YOUR OWN FOR YOU?

How do you know if *you* could make it? First, you have to have the desire to be your own boss and you have to believe in your capabilities to do it. Plus have talent, experience (go with what you know), salesmanship, tenacity, an instinct for what the market wants (not just what the market needs), money to get started with and survive through peaks and valleys, and luck—lots of luck—and probably a PC, printer, fax, software, copier, at least two phone lines, and a desk.

You shouldn't underestimate the difficulty of starting your own business. It will always take longer, cost more, and earn less than you think it should. On the other hand, it can provide more personal satisfaction, professional growth, and work security than you ever dreamed.

In 1995, over three hundred thousand Americans started their own business—a number that increases each year. *Newsweek* calls the self-employed "the new glamour profession."

Census statistics predict that by the year 2010, 60 percent of American jobs will be self-employed. Today nearly twenty-five million Americans (including part-time moonlighters) run a home business. And 1.7 million of them earn $100K a year, according to *Money* magazine.*

***Money* magazine statistics show that 63 percent are men, 37 percent women. Typically around forty-nine years old. Twice as likely to have a college degree than the average adult. The majority were paid about $45K in their old jobs and, on average, earn $58K as a full-time home-business owner. But it's not uncommon to find six- and seven-figure incomes among people working at home.

Why the Increase of Self-Employed?

Self-employed $100K Club members started their own company for many different reasons:

- "I was fired, unsuccessful at job hunting, and needed some work. So I decided to take a better offer than what I was getting out there—from myself."
- "I guess you'd say I was a born risk-taker. It's a source of pride to me to build a new business."
- "I didn't want to do any more of what I was sick of doing."
- "There was an opportunity my employer was missing. I saw it and decided to take it."
- "I was a new mother and wanted to spend more time at home. And I wanted something more gratifying than I had at the office."
- "With a telephone, fax machine, and computer, one can work anywhere."
- "I wanted my freedom."

A high proportion of people start their own business *after getting fired* (or a nicer word is *downsized*). Rather than looking for another job in which they'll be at the mercy of a boss and possibly lose another job, they start their own business.

That's what I did, and it turned out like the old standard cliché: It's the best thing that ever could have happened to me. I echoed what many entrepreneurs say: "I never want to have my job security controlled by anyone else ever again!"

The disadvantage of starting a new operation after losing a job is that sometimes the motivation is tension-releasing rather than goal-achieving. Meaning if your motivation for self-employment is desperation and/or revenge, you will likely fail. You have to *want* to be self-employed and be willing to release the security of a corporate job. If you already know you want to be on your own and a job termination just pushes up your timetable, well that's okay. It will be a good time to set out on your own.

A department head at the National Academy of Sciences anticipated a personality clash with the new department leader. So he quit rather than be fired. He then spent the weekend with three friends and several bottles of wine to brainstorm business ideas. Today he runs one of those business ideas on a Web site earning a seven-figure income.

Some people are just born risk-takers and they want an (almost) complete freedom to make mistakes—something they think they can do in their own business. In actuality, you can afford *fewer* mistakes in your own business than allowed in a corporate structure—where mistakes can easily be hidden or passed on to someone else. In your own business, the advantage is you can't get fired for your mistakes. (You may go bankrupt, but you probably won't dismiss yourself!)

Successful self-employed risk-takers make the inevitable mistakes and are willing to pay the price, monetarily or emotionally. And they have chosen now rather than later to have autonomy, control, be in charge, and have a say.

(Note: I don't deny one needs to be a risk-taker to try to climb up a corporate mountain. It's just a different risk, cost, and outcome.)

People start their own business because they simply see the opportunity to offer competitive services or products. (Like the man fulfilling repair part orders out of his garage.) They can be more flexible than big corporations, and with lower overhead for office space, salary, and smaller staff, they can offer competitive prices too.

In the corporate world, vision (that is, seeing opportunity) is prized among leaders. In the self-employment world, an individual simply directs his vision toward his future instead of a corporation's future. The people who founded UPS, Snapple, and Starbucks, for example, saw their chance.

Sometimes seeing opportunity means seeing the *lack* of opportunity, such as limits on compensation, slim annual raises, mergers, and acquisitions that affect you. If you've stayed aware of all going on around you, your department, company, and industry (as discussed in the chapter on making $100K in a corporate job), you can be just as clear as top management about potential in the marketplace.

In many situations you are easily as capable of seizing the opportunity as a big company is—if you've also followed the other steps outlined in this chapter. What you offer in terms of flexibility, creativity, energy, tenacity, and passion may offset what a big company machine has to offer in terms of money and staff size.

And then there are those long-term, successful "wage slaves" (as one executive described himself) who have earned lots of money and plainly see an opportunity to take advantage of tax laws for the self-employed.

Spending more time at home and around family is another motivation for starting a business. There are people who've gotten tired of commuting, for example, and have decided they want to be able to work in their pajamas and bunny slippers if they desire. The reality is, if they are successful, they won't end up working *fewer* hours. They will just be working more of them around the house.

The spouse of an entrepreneur once told me, "Sure he's home, but the telephone is always ringing, he's wheeling and dealing, and his mind isn't here." Being at home doesn't make your work life simpler; it can make it more complicated.

Like everything in life, there is a good and a bad side. The bad side of working at home is that family members see you and therefore think they have access to you, and interrupt. (And it's true that some aspiring entrepreneurs can't discipline *themselves* to demand the uninterrupted time they need. It's not the family members' problem, it's theirs.) You simply have to describe, and get an agreement on, ground rules of home-office behavior early on. For example:

- When the door is closed, do not disturb. When it's open, come in as much as you want.
- To get my attention when I'm busy, knock twice, or buzz me on the phone intercom system.
- Noon to 1 P.M. the office is closed every day. (Don't eat lunch in there. Don't watch television in there. Don't play video games. Don't do anything you wouldn't do at the office.)

The good side of working at home (or on your own) is that some family members eagerly become helpers. Spouse, children, in-laws, and neighbors have been known (free of charge) to label and stuff envelopes, make shipping boxes, type or proof letters, deliver product, pick up inventory at the airport, wait for expected phone calls, make phone calls, direct repair people, file material, organize storage, fulfill orders, and a myriad of other day-to-day activities. Your work team becomes your "home team" and tremendous group energy goes toward your goals. (It's one way you truly can spend more time with the family while building a business.)

Today, the biggest boon to the self-employed is *technology.* It allows small businesses to compete with big businesses by way of cellular phones, laptop computer-modem links for data transmission and printers, fax capabilities, voice mail, two-way message pagers, and other gadgets. This technology allows the entrepreneur to broaden sales and service areas without adding office and personnel costs.

A customer can't tell if your business is one month or ten years old.

For example, an individual can get a "domain address" (better known as E-mail address; for example, http://www.faccet.com/faucet/)* and can be all set in business and ready to sell something. The World Wide Web makes it easy for newcomers to market customer service, computer equipment, insurance, research, candy, clothing, communications programs, sex, and any other product or service that can be displayed for sale.

Big companies get the same type of address that small companies do, so big companies have no natural advantage. Browsers can't tell the difference between a giant corporation or one run on the back porch.

Electronic-mail technology is one of the most valuable Internet tools. It can reduce long-distance telephone and postage costs, plus it can provide customer service and marketing support.

The equipment needn't even take up your home space—you can outfit a van with a desk, chairs, files, a cellular phone, a laptop with modem, a printer, a fax machine, and a cordless extension phone. A workstation can fit into a briefcase.

Regardless of the reason for starting your own busi-

*In 1996, thirty-seven million people in the United States and Canada had access to the Net according to a Nielsen survey. They spent an average of 5.5 hours a week on-line. Two and a half million people have already made one or more purchases using the computer network.

According to *Nation's Business,* the Internet is growing at a rate of more than 10 percent a month; the business portion continues to expand even faster. Twenty-five thousand companies are listed in Yahoo, a widely used commercial Internet directory.

ness—you lost a job, you see an opportunity, you want time with family, you're willing to risk—a universal benefit is that you can meet your old boss at the mall and *not* have to laugh at his jokes. And that one benefit alone outweighs some minor disadvantages like: no paid vacations.

SO WHAT IS REQUIRED TO "DO YOUR OWN THING"—TO BECOME A SELF-EMPLOYED ENTREPRENEUR?

- Decide on your niche.
- Get started.
- Don't waste time.
- Believe in yourself and your goal.
- Make the tough decisions necessary.

Decide on Your Niche

Ernie Howell, a retired CEO, counseled me twenty years ago, "Provide what the market wants, *not* just what you want to do." If you don't fill a need, you will fail regardless of how well you execute your plans.

How do you determine what the market wants? Listen, watch, intelligently observe, read, ask knowledgeable people at every opportunity you get. When you've narrowed down some ideas, then pass them by your mentors. Keep in mind, they are going to point out potential problems, because that's part of their role—to help you make good decisions. Consider their opinions, but don't let them needlessly discourage you from carving out your niche.

Do not make your move into self-employment until you've learned all you can about business from your employers. It's a free education that is every bit as valuable as your formal education. One $100K Club member explained how he took advantage of the corporate education: "I quit my jobs every two years for eight years in a row to keep learning and growing in new areas. I sort of forced them to teach me everything they could before I'd move on."

CEO Curt Carter of Mission Bay Investments told me, "Debra, the goal is wrong for your readers if it is just to make money. That is an incorrect premise to work under. They will almost always be doomed to fail. If they're on their own for *other* reasons, it can lead to success. Reasons might be: They don't want to work for someone else, they have a great idea, or they want to do something they enjoy. . . . It's easy to make money if it's not what you set out to do. Tell your own story, Debra. You have a typical experience your readers can benefit from in how you developed your niche." (At the end of this chapter I follow his suggestion.)

Of course, despite the desire to do your own thing, you have to look to the current market for needs. Avoid going after any definite, and usually limited, trend.

In 1996, according to the American Home Business Association and the National Association of the Self-employed, the top business trends for earning $100K at home were:

- Export agent
- Employee trainer
- Management consultant
- Commercial debt negotiator
- Desktop video publisher
- Computer trainer and tutor
- Mailing list service provider
- Home inspector
- Temporary help provider

If you pick a current trend or "hot" area to get into, anticipate and prepare for it to die out. It likely will. Better to build an interest that lasts through what's "in" and "out"—something that satisfies your alls. (That's where the money is.) Build on your own skills and work experience rather than to go with a trend.

When you build a business using your own ideas and skills, you'll have more satisfying and ultimately long-term profitable work.

Thousands will nonetheless choose a franchise or buy a going business. It's easier than starting from scratch and financially more accessible. If the franchise operation fits their all, it can turn out to be a very good decision. If not, it will be a costly decision.

Be aware there are many scam artists (often self-employed) plying on your self-employment dreams and trying to get *your* savings into *their* bank account. An example is most franchise organizations requiring only a "$495 initiation fee." (The FTC requires franchisers who charge $500 or more to file disclosure documents that must include the franchiser's background, with names and addresses of other franchisees. The required documentation likely makes for a more reliable franchise.)

Three-fourths of the people who buy a business (according to *Inc.* magazine) have the financial resources to get into one and feel their management talent is transferable despite their inexperience in the field. A lawyer who advises people on buying businesses, Dennis O'Connor, says, "The business is going to be much more challenging in terms of time than they ever expected, and they won't get financial rewards in line with the effort they put in. It never ends, and it's brutal. If you're working for yourself and doing something you like, it can offset that. But meeting payroll is one of the toughest things in the work, and it doesn't go away."

Here is a list to give you an idea of purchase costs of businesses recently for sale:

- A Seattle bookstore: $62,000
- An Arizona AM-radio station: $650,000
- A California comedy club: $350,000

- A Texas dragstrip: $500,000
- A Virginia French bakery: $275,000
- A Florida travel agency: $150,000
- A Nevada casino: $2,300,000
- A North Carolina motorcycle dealership: $1,100,000
- An Arizona bowling center: $3,600,000
- A Washington ski mountain: best offer

(A big caution concerning buying an ongoing business: You inherit facilities, equipment, employees, ***and*** attitude, customers, and problems.)

There are lots of books about franchise businesses, if you're interested. My purpose here is just to point these out as self-employment options. Regardless of the direction you choose, the steps laid out for success and the avenues to avoid for failure remain the same.

A good way to get your feet wet in your own venture is to moonlight in a business you're considering buying or starting. Try out your niche on small projects while still enjoying the financial security of a salaried employee. You can also test what the market wants during a moonlighting phase.

Hewlett-Packard is just one company that spawns a number of home-based businesses because many projects can easily be handled by outside consultants. After employees experience the ability to moonlight with company-sponsored work, they sometimes quit the company to turn around and provide the same services back to their former employer.

The company ends up with less overhead, yet still gets the same work done.

The employee ends up with more money* because her hourly rate can surpass what she was earning while employed. She has self-employment tax write-offs, so she ends up getting more money for the same work—on her own. Plus, by being a former insider, she is known, her work likely meets their standard, and it makes for easier marketing to other customers.

Unless you work under a "no compete" contract, almost any work you're doing as an employee can be done on a moonlighting basis. Obviously you have to consider the potential for conflict of interest and guard against that happening. You don't need your venture into self-employment soiled with a lawsuit from a former employer.

As you develop your niche, don't limit yourself to just what you already know. You can learn new areas or hire other at-home specialists to supplement your expertise. The health food newsletter editor mentioned earlier hired a trade show expert as he entered into that business, and he consulted a Soviet relations expert before getting into the Soviet plywood business.

When you develop and go after your niche, you will

*The company saves money while the employee ends up with more. How? Hewitt Associates calculates 40 percent of employees' salary consists of benefits. In other words, with what the company saves in benefits, it can pay the new "outsider" a higher hourly rate, and they both end up better off. Of course, the new entrepreneur will have to start paying for the benefits out of her own pocket. (Exact numbers need to be worked out with an accountant before making any drastic decision, of course.)

experience satisfaction unlike any time in your adult life. "Every single day I have the feeling 'How can I possibly be this happy,' " says Dennis Hoppe, president of Hoppe Management Concepts. But you have to get started to experience that glee.

Get Started

Getting started means you need to arrange funding, set up accounting systems, purchase health and maybe disability and life insurance, acquire office equipment, and check local ordinances and regulations. (Some communities limit the number of employees or number of client visits you can have in a certain time period in a residential area, for example).

If you're going for bank or outside financing, you'll need to write a well-thought-out business plan including start-up costs, operating expenses, and projected income. The characteristics of a successful plan:

- *Clear, realistic financial projections.* A narrative should accompany performance to date, cash flow, income statement, and balance-sheet forecasts.
- *Detailed market research.* Demonstrate that you know your customers and the problems you are solving. Most importantly, what makes you think that you'll succeed where so many have failed?
- *Detailed competitor research.* Learn everything

you can about competitors' product, pricing, promotion, employees, and overall success.

- *Management.* Have a strong management team with no holes.
- *A great summary.* The reader needs a summary of your business at a glance: what you're seeking, the market, the company's management, and the product.
- *Proof of vision.* Have enough detail to demonstrate you know goals are attainable.
- *Good formatting and clear writing.* Be sure your plan is interesting to read, well-written, and smooth-flowing. Write short paragraphs and use bullet points wherever applicable.
- *Keep the plan short.* Fewer than forty pages is a good goal.
- *Design for the bottom line.* Explain clearly why you need financing, what kind of financing best suits the company, and how the bank or investor will be repaid.
- *Make the plan your own.* Always create the plan by yourself first, before going to a professional. Professionals can point out the weak points, but you want *your* thoughts down, not the professionals'. (For more information, refer to *Nation's Business* magazine. They do a good job providing critical details.)

Whether your entrepreneurial venture is acquired or dreamed up, you also have to decide how you're going to market your business. Create self-promotional materials. Establish yourself as an expert. Increase your visibility. Differentiate yourself from the competition. Generate media interest in your business and become newsworthy. (Marketing is *one* part of selling.)

Financial experts say you should have six months of personal living expenses set aside. $100K Club members who've started their own business recommend twelve months. In your own business, you might end up making bigger money faster than you ever have in your life. But you'll likely be spending bigger money faster than you ever have in your life—and every dollar will be coming out of your pocket.

Most at-home businesses self-finance or get financial help from family or friends. In addition to living expenses, estimates are you'll need $4K to $10K for the basic office equipment—which may include computer with modem, fax machine, laser-quality printer, and telephone answering system.

Many business opportunities don't require that kind of equipment. The carpenter may need tools and a pickup truck. The classical music producer requires professional recording equipment.

Getting started doesn't only mean setting up shop. It means *today,* several years before you plan to hang out your shingle, you start researching what the market wants and needs that you could provide. Get started on a trial business plan to see how numbers fall out so you can start budgeting now. Get started on learning how competitors market their product or service. Get started on every aspect of your dream business *now,* long before you actually make a break for it.

Your success will be in direct proportion to your thinking, planning, dreaming, and researching—all put in long before you actually start.

Don't Waste Time

Even if your own business is only a faint possibility now, don't waste time starting to plan, think about, dream about, and work toward it. You can always scrap your plans. But in the meantime:

- You'll keep your creative juices flowing.
- You'll maintain a better attitude because you always have something else to fall back on.
- You might come up with an idea you can sell to your employer, become a hero, and get promoted.
- You could come up with something so fantastic you can't waste any more time employed!

$100K Club members emphasize: Don't waste time making a decision to go out on your own. That does not mean leaving your job before being prepared. Prepare by learning all you can from your employer; maybe try a venture on a trial level, or moonlight.

And the moment you hang out your shingle, you can't waste your time on anything but getting work or performing the work. If it takes you three days to write a proposal, that may need to change to three hours.

Every day you procrastinate making an important phone call will put you a month deeper in debt. If you dread selling, change that attitude and *read* fourteen books on the subject this month. If you can't bring yourself to do that, don't go into business for yourself.

In an entrepreneurial situation, your entire life has to be disciplined. And you have to be a disciplined self-starter. (You can't imagine how easy it is to fall into a sense of complacency.) You can't waste time, effort, energy, or money on whims and whatever you *feel* like. Every resource available to you has to be expensed with discipline.

When you're on your own, you learn to "pick up the mirror and talk to your staff about what needs to be done today—and do it," as Paul Schlossberg, president of Dallas-based D/FW Consulting, put it.

"Every night I make a list of what I'll do tomorrow, including taking the dog for a walk. I prioritize it. I have the option of doing anything I want because I'm my own boss, but I know I'll pay penance for it. I learned my first week out, if you're working out of your home, you can't go watch daytime talk shows!" said Inge Trump of Trump Property Management in Denver.

A small action that saves time for Paul Schlossberg: He addresses and stamps an envelope before he goes to meet a client. After the meeting, all he has to do is insert a note to complete his follow-up. This action minimizes the possibility that he'll forget this important step and prompts him to write the note while the details of the meeting are still fresh in his mind.

Unfortunately, you can waste time while *doing* business. A New York journalist who works at home explains how lunch can take four hours: getting dressed, putting on makeup, leaving the house, going downtown, coming home, getting undressed, and answering calls missed when she was out.

Conserve the limited time you have by choosing the right activities to be involved in and people to be around. That's self-discipline.

Don't waste precious time before starting to lay the groundwork. Start now. None of the $100K Club members I've talked to said they started their own business too early.

Believe in Yourself and Your Goal

You have to be an unfailingly disciplined optimist. If you do not maintain a positive outlook, you'll have a major problem. The whole operation travels on your back. Fact is, you need to be optimistic to keep yourself up too. If you aren't a disciplined optimist, everyone around you gets down when you get down.

Along with self-discipline is self-motivation. It's critical. You have no one to answer to except yourself and the bill collector; no one is looking over your shoulder. The freedom is tremendously burdensome.

Action is the word to remember: "I need to get it done. I need to make it happen. I need to be flexible. I need to do something now." This must be your mantra.

You can only take effective action when you believe in what you're doing. Don't make the mistake of thinking everyone who ever started his own enterprise was one hundred percent competent, confident, and comfortable in his decisions. *No one ever is.* But while they might not have believed they were so special, they did believe in the product or service and had enough confidence to be the one to bring it forth. They had faith in their abilities because they knew they'd work like the devil to get done whatever needed to be done.

My recommendation is:

- Back up your belief in yourself with preparation and homework.
- Then strike out and do what needs to be done.
- And keep at it.

Why harp on self-discipline, motivation, action? Because *you're* responsible. Responsible for getting work done. Responsible for managing others. Responsible for vision. You can't hide from mistakes made when you're on your own.

Make the Tough Decisions Necessary

Leaving a corporate job is a tough decision. Starting your own business is a tough decision. Turning down bad business is one also. The tough decisions you're required to make are endless. Get used to it.

You need to be able to take a look at your balance sheet on a regular basis and see if you are where you thought you'd be. Then, if not, acknowledge and fix it, or move on if you can't. You need to constantly think what can improve the product, what can improve the service—because the competition is asking those same questions. (It takes ten times the selling costs to get a new client than it does to keep an old one.)

Cut your losses. If you aren't in the right business, even though it is your own, do something different. Start another company. Don't be guilty of getting deeper into something you're not good at.

Nobody is there to give a negative performance appraisal. You have to see it, admit it, and think of some new business or direction.

If the business grows, you'll start having the same situation you left in the corporate world. All the complaints you had about management may now be aimed at *you.* You have no one to blame but yourself and, what's more, everyone has you to blame too for the tough decisions.

That's a basic foundation for starting your own business.

Now you want to make it into the six-figure arena.

BREAKING THE $100K MARK

So many factors will affect your success: motivation going in, the idea you have, execution of plans, luck, market, timing, and other things you can't always anticipate. One factor that will carry a large part of your success is your personal ability (and willingness) to sell both yourself and your product or service.

First Rule of Self-Employment: You're in Sales

If you're self-employed, you're in sales. You absolutely have to be able to sell yourself and your product or service. If you aren't willing to talk to strangers and try to convince them to buy what you have to offer, then you better stay employed elsewhere. Every bit of success depends on *you* being persuasive to financiers, customers, employees, vendors, the media, your family, and yourself.

Take on a salesperson approach in whatever work you are currently doing—for practice. How do you learn to sell while still employed when that isn't your job? Be willing to learn. Read books, attend seminars, talk with salespeople. Identify customers who are the most successful users of your product (or others') and find out why they buy. Ask what they look for in a salesperson. Practice what you learn by selling an idea to your boss, spouse, child, or friend. You don't have to *like* this part of your job, you just have to do it.

Being a salesperson is partially being a problem solver—also, a priority setter with street smarts and raw intelligence added. Selling is the ability to read other people, persuade them, and enthuse them to your point of view.

Selling is a form of office politics—you have to get along with customers, suppliers, competitors. No, you don't have to kiss up. But you do have to be sensible, courteous, and forthright.

That's what selling is all about: It's selling yourself as well as your product or service.

At the start of your own business, you will have to be the product developer, bookkeeper, salesperson, and stamp licker. (Fortunately, not boot licker.) You must deal with every problem—you can't say, "It's not my job." After a period of time, you'll discover what you truly are best at and the reason you started your own business. You can concentrate on what you like and hire a freelancer to do the part you don't like—such as bookkeeping or advertising. The one area you can never abdicate, though, is selling.

Second Rule of Self-Employment: You Will Work Harder than You Ever Have in Your Life.

But the good side is, it's all to your benefit.

You have to work very hard. As Don Goings, a business partner at Sulcus, says, "The most money is made *after* five P.M."

I was talking to Nancy Albertini, CEO of Dallas-based Taylor-Winfield, when she told me about that week's schedule: "I just got back from a four-hour meeting in Paris. I arrived in the morning, attended the meeting, set up a European contact, and returned home the same day." I commented about her seventy-hour workweeks and she replied, "Debra, we *aren't* part-time, you know!"

In your own business, time will tend to be less balanced because nobody is there to help you. You do it on your own. More work time will be put in (now and forever) when you're on your own—and that's okay because it is all to your benefit.

Jack Southard told me about his first three years in business: "I didn't take a day off, not Thanksgiving, Easter, or Christmas. I kept expenses down by doing most of the work myself. The satisfaction of doing my own work was worth it, though."

Frankly, you have to sell and you have to work hard when in your own business. There is no way around it if you want to make big money.

But other than that, the worst part of being your own boss is that when you call in sick, you know you're lying. And when you downsize, it means replacing yourself with someone better!

I truly cannot count the number of people who have told me, "It's easy to make a six-figure income in your own enterprise." And when I ask "How?" they answer with: Find your niche, get started, don't waste time, take risks, make the tough decisions, believe in yourself, work *really* hard.

There are people who aren't ready for being on their own yet, but do see a need to get out of the corporate environment. An option for those people might be telecommuting.

The Telecommuter

Telecommuting is a reasonable "bridge" between a corporate job and full self-employment. One week a month or one day a week spent working out of your home gives you a taste of doing your own thing. Although you may still be working for someone else, you're away from the corporate situation and disciplines. It's a good way to test your ability to optimistically maintain self-motivation and discipline, test decision making, and avoid wasting time.

Six million Americans now telecommute an average of one and a half days a week. A technology research firm, Find/SVP, predicts that 10 percent of the work-force will be telecommuting by the year 2000. Aside from assembly-line work, most anything else can be done away from a corporate office with a PC, modem, on-line services, and a telephone system.

The benefits of telecommuting (as well as working at home) are:

- Fewer distractions
- Closer to the field (or customer)
- More objectivity
- Relaxed environment

Fewer Distractions. In an office there are masses of people around. People and activities that interrupt your work, delay deadlines, and derail priorities. At home, at least the number of people you have to deal with is smaller—the family and the pets.

"I'm an early riser. I get up at four every morning. Between four and eight I get a full day's work done with no interruptions," says Motorola manager Dave Fults.

Closer to the Field (or Customer). Sales and service people, for example, need to be close to the customer. The sooner you are able to solve a customer's problem, the happier the customer, and often that means being on-site quickly.

Michael Christman is a regional manager for Lifetouch National Studios. They take photographs of children at department stores, plus school and church members' photos. He says, "Living in the region I service lets me better represent the field to my company, and my company to the field, because I'm physically there instead of my corporate office."

More Objectivity. A person away from the mainstream of activity is more autonomous, more objective. When you are working in the middle of things, you can get too focused on the corporate perspective versus the customer's perspective.

A telecommunications regional manager bought a thirty-five-foot recreational vehicle and outfitted it with his electronic gear. He said, "After finishing a five-day trade show in Las Vegas, I drove a day to Yuma and made a sales call. Drove another day to Phoenix and made three sales calls. There wasn't anything I couldn't do in that vehicle that was normally done at the office. The company paid my mileage, meals, and camping hookups, plus my wife got to go along. By being accessible, I was able to fully service the customer and, at the same time, not worry about what was going on at the office so much."

More Relaxed Environment. It takes personal discipline, but an individual can stay more focused on her work if she is in a relaxed environment not full of office tensions and distractions.

One regional manager who works part-time out of his home and part-time out of an office suite away from the company office says, "I decide what I'll focus on and when. If I'm in the mood not to answer phone calls, that is what I do. I go with how I feel and therefore I deliver better performance. I'm considering buying a boat and using it as an office. I saw an attorney in San Diego who had his shingle hanging on a pole at his boat slip. One would have to be able to justify it, of course, keep a log, and hook up by satellite. But that would be a great environment to work out of."

Michael Christman says he can sit around in workout clothes and get things done. Every couple of hours he takes fifteen minutes and works out on his home exercise equipment. "I don't need to dress up to do what I need to. Then I can save good clothes for when I go out on the road."

More relaxed doesn't mean being lazy about work. In fact, one thing I've found in common among $100K Club members is that they are never "on vacation." Meaning regardless of where they are—on a boat, at the gym, in the car, on a plane, at the theater, anywhere—they are always working something in their mind as it relates to their all and their work.

When structured in a thought-out manner, companies save money and employees save time working outside of the office. Not the least of the benefits to society is cleaner air due to less auto pollution from long commutes.

There are disadvantages of telecommuting as well:

- Job expansion
- The "Out of sight, out of mind" possibility
- Distractions

Job Expansion. You have to solve different types of problems than just your own work. Say the copier runs out of paper or breaks down. At the office someone takes care of that. On your own, you do.

The resources (such as people, equipment, and data) ready at hand at the office aren't at home. More effort goes into accessing them or even creating them yourself.

The "Out of Sight, Out of Mind" Possibility. It is true that if the boss doesn't see you or hear from you, she may forget about you. You have to put more effort into staying in touch. Electronic-mail and faxes make it technologically possible, but other kinds of efforts are required as well.

Arrange to talk in person, or at least on the telephone, with your boss three times a week for thirty minutes each time. Have it put on her calendar like any other appointment. Keep a list of things to talk about, and prioritize them in case you don't get through all of them.

If a boss doesn't have ready access to you—for either your talent or your point of view—she might stop counting on it. Also, when you aren't in the loop, you can miss out on changes in thinking. A new shift that occurred at noon may not be communicated to you till two weeks later. Then the boss says, "Oh, did I forget to tell you?" (Yet I've seen departments in corporate headquarters, located only thirty feet apart from each other in the same building, that didn't know what was going on between them either!)

It is true that a lot of business decisions take place in casual office situations, business lunches, and during an after-work game of darts. Just like you schedule a "keep posted" phone meeting with your boss, you can find out when the gang is going to lunch or gathering at Joe's driveway basketball court—and be there too.

Distractions. Unless a spouse and children respect and agree with your work schedule demand, they may derail you. "My wife used to come in and ask, 'Can you do . . .' every hour of the day. She couldn't get used to the fact that since I was physically there I was available to her," said a man starting his own business.

One mother hired a nanny to care for her young children. They got the first floor and the backyard as their domain. She then organized a separate room that was somewhat isolated from the main area as her office. When she was in her office, she was off limits. But she also put on her calendar the two o'clock appointment to read her children a story before their nap. Later the family bought the house next door and made it her office.

A CEO told me he has started regular written correspondence to his kids. "I write letters in my business all the time explaining what we're doing, want to do, need from the reader, and so on. So I just decided to do the same for my kids, whom I don't get to spend that much time with. I tell them why I did certain things in my life, what I hope for them, what I think about current events, and general feelings on things. I hope it makes up for the lack of time with me."

Everything can be distracting if you are not self-disciplined—the laundry, the lawn, the television, the cat, the dog, and of course much more.

If you conclude the benefits of telecommuting outweigh the drawbacks, following are six suggestions to use when convincing your employer to let you telecommute:

1. Review your tasks and separate ones that must be done at the office from those that could be done away from the office. This helps determine the time split.
2. Consider your boss's job is to oversee. So suggest ways he can effectively keep an eye on you. Offer ideas on how you report completed work, for example. You can explain that the boss will have more free time to think and plan if not watchdogging.
3. Evaluate what equipment you will need. If the company isn't willing to pay for it, you may need to do it yourself.
4. Suggest a trial telecommute for both sides to see the benefits and the drawbacks. Something like a day a week for two to three months should be adequate time. Let your boss and your family know the trial period is just that—a trial. Your boss or you may decide it's not a good idea.

Women on maternity leave have found telecommuting extends their leave while still allowing them to get necessary work done.

5. Keep your boss informed of your work activity plans and progress. When you are "out of sight, out of mind," you might not get the memo on an important meeting. Remember, it's now your responsibility to make it easy for people to track you down. Be clear how you want to be kept posted and how you will keep others posted as well. You must put more effort than ever before into quantifying your contributions to the right people.
6. Communicate the fact that you will be putting in as many hours at home as at the office. The benefit is the flexibility of which hours you use, but it will take just as many—maybe more, if you add the time necessary to stay visible. Remember, it is your responsibility to make sure your work gets noticed and not allow "out of sight, out of mind."

Then, on your own, talk with your accountant about home-office and self-employment tax laws. And if you plan to work at home, check with your family to get cooperation in respecting your office time requirements while at home.

Why People Don't Succeed in Their Own Business

Business observers report there is a five-year mark when a business will either turn and do well or it won't. Statistics show that 70 percent of new businesses go broke within those five years.

Why do self-employment ventures fail? The top eight reasons:

1. The person is not prepared enough.
2. More management is required than the person is able to provide.
3. The person is too cautious and not enough of a risk-taker.
4. Finances aren't managed well.
5. There is a lack of discipline.
6. There is a lack of focus.
7. The person can't (or more likely *won't*) sell.
8. There are ego problems.

1. Companies fail because the founder hadn't learned enough about business in general before jumping ship. Perhaps good mentors were scarce for needed advice. Plans were not thought out well enough or were executed poorly. Strong business and personal management skills are obviously necessary. Sheer energy and enthusiasm, although great assets, are not sufficient.

2. The individual left a big business in which she was surrounded by staff and had deep-pocket spending power. The company she can afford to buy (or start) not only needs a president, but someone who can load the truck, sell, deal with bankers, get on the line and work, sweep the floor, and so forth. All of a sudden, instead of being a vice president of marketing, she is president, vice president, sales manager, salesperson, buyer, secretary, production worker, marketing, shipping, *and* janitorial. It's too much mentally and physically for some people.

The pool of resources to call on is limited when *you* are the company—unless you developed business friendships from various companies, industries, and disciplines long before starting on your own.

3. The person found out he wasn't the risk-taker he claimed to be. Many think they can succeed but they can't do anything without ten other people helping, supporting, and approving their work.

4. The person can't manage personal finances. Without financial staying power, new businesses don't last.

Just one example: New owners often don't realize the benefits they received while employed.* Remember

*Social Security taxes and Medicare taxes are 15.3 percent. As an employee you only pay half of that; your employer pays the other half. An employee earning $100K pays approximately $7,650 in Social Security and Medicare taxes, while a sole proprietor with the same income pays $12,152. And health insurance premiums for individual coverage go sky high with limited choices.

the fact that some 40 percent of your salary was benefits. Now you have to earn more than 140 percent your former salary to pay for benefits on your own. And small companies do not get the deals big companies do.

Staying within budget, keeping overhead low, not wasting money, not making mistakes that cost money, and delaying gratification are all part of managing business and personal finances.

5. The person can't discipline herself to get up, get dressed, go into her home office, and start to work. There's too much freedom.

Artist Scott Fraser does not wait until he gets inspired to work. He starts at eight A.M. five days a week. Works until noon. Starts again at one P.M. and goes until six. He does that five days a week, every week.

6. Some people can't stay focused. A zillion distractions occur as a matter of course, but unless your focused goal pervades everything, it will fall apart.

It could be like the Mercedes repairman in Denver. Lots of his well-heeled clients also own Lexuses and BMWs. They like his Mercedes repair work and constantly ask him to look at their other cars. He always (nicely) refuses. His focus is to be the best *Mercedes* mechanic that anyone can find in the city.

7. The person can't sell. (It's more likely he *won't* sell than can't.)

Everyone sells. You persuade your spouse, kids, friends to do things your way. You get consensus from fellow team members. You negotiate the sale of your house, a boat, a bike, or a car sometime in your life.

You clean out your garage at a yard sale. You convince the tailor to throw in an extra free alteration. You get rid of the litter of puppies. All of that is selling.

One lesson to take from this book is the need to sell yourself and your product inside and outside of the organization, up and down the ladder. If you can't or won't, you'll miss out on the big bucks. If you feel selling is beneath you, degrading, and nerve-wracking, you're sabotaging yourself with a destructive attitude.

You don't have to like it; you just have to do it, and do it well. John Downing, president of Downcourt Enterprises, *can* sell because he *has* to. He explained his methodical approach: First he sends a letter, brochure, and video to prospects using the name of the referral who gave the prospect's name. Three days later he sends a second video of follow-up material.

The first package is mailed so it arrives on Monday. The second one, so it arrives on Thursday. On the next Tuesday the prospect is called and asked if he's received the material, had a chance to review it, and would he set up an appointment. Usually the prospect recalls receiving it but hasn't reviewed it. The response is, "I'll call Monday at ten. Will you have time to review it and schedule a brief appointment?" Over 60 percent agree to his request.

His methodical, organized approach forces him to do what needs to be done.

8. And one of the greatest of all reasons at-home or entrepreneurial operations fail is ego. Donald Trump may claim "Every big vision is backed by ego" and be speaking a truth. But the truth is also that most failure is ego-driven: The person is afraid to do what needs to be done because

she is afraid of looking dumb and making mistakes. It takes a maverick streak in a person that doesn't let ego get in the way.

When you start your own business, your ego has to be put aside. Now you will be required to do too many things that were "beneath" you before. If you do what needs to be done without the ego getting in the way, you will have many opportunities for it to be satisfied later.

From experiences of $100K Club members I emphasize some cautions:

- Check with an insurance agent about homeowner's and auto coverage while pursuing business. Employees definitely won't be covered.
- Carry at least $1 million in liability insurance in addition to your property and casualty coverage.
- Before you quit your day job, budget for health insurance costs. It will be sky-high compared to your employer-paid insurance.
- Stay honest and timely in your dealings with employees, landlords, and the IRS.
- You'll soon discover managing one employee is as difficult as ten. Hire slowly and carefully. Turnover is a financial drain.

And now my story of how self-employment worked for me.

To my way of thinking, it doesn't get any better than this. To be able to support myself in the style I want without having to get along with a boss!

In April 1976, my manager at Control Data Corporation called me into his office to say the management trainee job I was hired for was not working out. I was given two months' severance pay.

Surprise, tears, disappointment, embarrassment, and worry all took over that day. But only that day. Numbness took over the next two days (fortunately Saturday and Sunday). By Monday I was ready to show them their mistake by doing great work somewhere else.

I went back to my boss and asked for double the severance. He countered with three months. At that time most people got two weeks; although I felt extremely lucky with two months, I also knew I had nothing to lose by asking for more—they couldn't fire me!

I then wrote a list of everything I had done in my life that I was proud of. (At age twenty-one, it wasn't a very long list.) Then I described what the situation was, what I had done well, and what resulted. I was looking for a pattern of accomplishment.

I found everything I liked to do was *on my own:* commission selling jobs in high school and college, windsurfing, autocrossing, beauty pageants. (Remember, the list was not lengthy.) Notice the similarity in each —*individual* activity.

Plus, both of my parents had been self-employed businesspeople. From before I was born they owned a "Ma and Pa" drugstore, then grocery store, and then dress shops. The businesses never grew to raging enterprises, but they always provided a good middle-class living for the family. My parents were always their own boss.

My individual activity, entrepreneurial upbringing, and the fact that I *never* wanted to be in a position to be fired again helped me decide to start my own business. I wanted security in myself because I knew there wasn't any in a company.

In July 1976 I started a company called All Around Girls. The purpose was to provide any "legal, moral, and ethical" services needed by businessmen. (At that time there were only business*men*—no *-women*—with enough reason or money to pay an outside source to do odd jobs.) The odd jobs were things like:

- Shopping for executive gifts at Christmas
- Party planning
- Inventorying stolen silverware and broken glasses after a party and resupplying the inventory
- Delivery services of cars to mechanics, dogs to groomers, clothes to laundry, et cetera
- Competitive research on businesses my clients were considering using
- A little surveillance on competition, ex-wives, et cetera
- Delivery of important documents to distant locations (this was before UPS)
- Special events management such as company picnics

In 1976, my hourly services fee was $15 plus out-of-pocket expenses. I soon realized I would never get wealthy doing this work, despite how much fun it was. I also found I liked dealing with people in authority.

Nonetheless, at twenty-one I was a business owner, and other people started asking me advice. I liked giving advice.

By late 1976 I started a different company: Benton Management Resources. The idea of a company named after myself was very attractive. Plus the name was still general enough to provide any service I could successfully sell.

At that time there was a new industry just starting out West, where I lived. To my observation and study it required tenacity, creativity, resourcefulness, organization, and sales ability. It didn't require a specific degree or work record. It was called outplacement. Outplacement is a form of career counseling in which a person's strengths and weaknesses are analyzed to better market them for a new job. A terminated employee will often have this service paid for by the company that let them go, which undertakes this expense to get the person off unemployment earlier, to ease the employer's guilt for firing a worker, and to minimize the possibility of a legal action for unlawful termination. Today the business has evolved into a highly specialized human resource function.

Since I wasn't really qualified for anything, but did have the work traits listed, and the business didn't require much overhead, OUTPLACEMENT is what my company shingle was to read.

It turned out that a new business in a blossoming industry, run by a woman, in a new geographic territory, was attractive—not only to the media but to big companies back East.

Once I got my market research done, brochure written, program organized, and started selling, I was in business. Companies like Union Carbide, True Value, Citicorp, and Del Monte became clients.

It was a good business financially, but I could see after about five years that I was tired of counseling fired people.

In the back of my mind remained a personal interest of mine: the "chemistry factor" in business. You know, the intangible thing you can't quite put your finger on but it seems to make or break a career.

In moonlighting fashion I started studying what it was that set two comparably skilled people apart. What made one flounder and one soar. I was interested in the results of the study for myself, not necessarily for others.

I liked what I was learning, so I started volunteering to give free talks to local clubs. They started asking me back. I decided to charge the second time. They kept asking.

One day I called Bob Greene of the *Chicago Tribune* and told him I might have some research that would be of interest to his readers. He agreed to talk with me and ended up writing a column about "Debra Benton of Benton Management Resources, who teaches *charisma.*"

I had never made that claim, nor thought of myself in that way. I called it Executive Effectiveness.

The day the *Chicago Tribune* article ran, both *Newsweek* and *Time* magazine called to do a story. Only *Time* came through.

When the *Time* article was printed, three company presidents called me for consulting assignments along with a New York meeting organizer. In exchange for my speaking for a modest fee, he would invite the media. The *New York Times* and *Barron's* showed, and each did a half-page article. (I should note that President Reagan was in office and executive charisma was a big item, and here was a woman the press said could teach it!)

After the *New York Times* article was printed, *CBS Morning News* with Diane Sawyer called for me to be a guest, followed by *Good Morning America* and the *Today Show.* Unbeknownst to me, the *New York Times* and *Time* magazine articles were printed in the international editions.

I started getting calls from Germany, Iceland, France, England, Australia. An article in a Johannesburg paper read something like: "You've all heard of Harvard in the United States, the best school in the country. . . . Now there is a small school in Ft. Collins, Colorado, that teaches . . ."

Another surprise came when someone called about the article he read in *Playboy*! I hadn't interviewed for the South African paper or *Playboy.* I'm not complaining but just setting the record straight. I learned that the press can make you and, of course, it can break you.

Keep in mind that if I wasn't offering good advice, none of this would have happened. If I hadn't taken the initiative to call Bob Greene, none of this would have happened. But fortunately for me, a lot did happen that I didn't have anything to do with—it was just luck, timing, tenacity, willingness to work hard, and willingness to sell.

A French communications company sent someone to my offices in Colorado to negotiate a license contract for my services in Europe. During one of my business introductory trips to Paris, the publication *Le Figaro* printed headlines touting THE AMERICAN WOMAN TEACHING FRENCH CHARISMA!

Prospective clients called me instead of me calling them. My business started growing through referrals. When a senior executive felt he benefited, he told a friend, who signed up also.

Up to this point in this brief recap, I've made it sound pretty easy—but let me make clear the other side. I worked all the time, from sunup to sundown—seven days a week. My only break was to eat and exercise. I made sure to do both. I developed no new friends—there was no time for them. Frequently my parents didn't see me as much as they liked.

Every vacation, if there was one, was based on a business trip. Every clothing item I bought was with a business consideration in mind. I had no hobbies, barely watched television—ate, slept, breathed business from age twenty-one on. Business was my life; that's all I knew.

But it's all I wanted to know, because I realized to compete with the big boys I had to be not just as good, but better, because I was a young female.

Although there were many successes, there were many setbacks. Despite relatively low overhead, I cleared only $2,000 one year. Break-even!

But I never gave up on myself. I had some natural talent and developed experience to supplement it. I sold all day long to everybody. I was tenacious. I found something that I liked to do and that the market wanted. I kept overhead extremely low and I was *darn lucky.*

The media blitz hit in the mid-eighties. My client base grew and I was able to be selective about who I worked with (selective, not snobbish) and was able to raise my fees several thousand dollars higher. (I found that nothing accelerates the learning process like clients putting money on the line.)

I began getting assignments in different parts of the world—seventeen different countries in all.

With each year comes new experiences, clients, and opportunities. I've counseled a man running for the office of U.S. president plus numerous other politicians, prepared an individual to job interview with Donald Trump, and coached a person making his first Academy Award appearance. I've worked with numerous CEOs in preparing for stockholder meetings and investor road shows, consulted to thousands of executives and managers wanting to make their way to the top of their company, or the top of the field in their own company. Every week someone

I've worked with, coached, counseled, mentored (or who mentored me) is on the pages of *Forbes* and *Fortune.*

I have a tremendous job: I talk with interesting people all day long, learn about them and their work, provide advice to them, and get paid for it! Ninety percent of my business comes from referrals, the rest from the books or articles. Today I don't have to make those twenty-five telephone calls a day, but if necessary I could and would. I'm just as tenacious today as I was in 1976, but I'm more effective in my efforts.

And remember the company that fired me because I didn't fit in? They later became a client.

My story is typical of anyone who has worked hard—following her heart—with some degree of talent, experience, a willingness to sell, and tenacity to keep at it.

You can have an even better story—depending on your goals, talents, belief in yourself, tenacity, willingness to risk, ability to make decisions, avoidance of wasting time, and desire to keep job security under your control, not someone else's.

Whether you make the $100K mark by being your own boss or working from a corporate office, there are benefits—and costs. The next chapter prepares you for what to expect as a six- figure income earner.

"Earning a six-figure income takes commitment, some time, and a lot of hard work. If your work is personally rewarding and you do it well, the financial rewards will follow. With it comes the freedom to stay with your job because you want to; not because you need to."

—CECILIA HABERZETTL, Ph.D.
Assistant Director, Centocor

"Once people learn they can live with what they may see as a contradiction—a comfortable and pleasant lifestyle combined with actions and social justice concerns—they will experience the freedom of independence.

"You need to have a risk-taking mentality. Frame your bet. Understand your risk. Use judgment. Trust your instincts.

"What goes around comes back to haunt you. Have integrity and be trustworthy. Have humility. Arrogance is a turn-off.

"Speak clearly."

—SCOTT BALL,
Sales Manager, Koch Industries

"Develop comfort with numbers. Even if your job is in sales, advertising, or law, a mile away from the numbers crunchers, you need to understand that the performance of a company is, in the end, still measured with numbers.

"Whether with your customers, vendors, supervisors, or subordinates, put conflicts and problems on the table, deal with them, and move on. Having the courage and maturity to confront shortcomings and mistakes quickly is a sign that you are ready to move up.

"As unfair as it seems, many times there is no difference between competence and the perception of competence. People rise in organizations based on perceptions. Those that cultivate positive perceptions gain an advantage. (The same is true for 'connections.')"

—J. STANLEY PAYNE,
Corporate Vice President,
Bassett

CHAPTER 7

What $100K Buys You (And Costs You)

"Money isn't everything," says a man I know, with total honesty. "But until that day when I do have everything, I'll take money."

This is not to say that wealth is synonymous with success, either personal or professional. In reality, there is only one success, and that is to be able to spend your life in your own way.

The benefits, of course, to be obtained from a fulfilling business career are obvious. But making big money is a lot like playing golf and making a hole in one—you may be required to pay for drinks for everyone in the clubhouse! Money does provide you with many wonderful things . . . and (like the good news/bad news cliché) it costs you as well.

THE BENEFITS

Although we know wealth is not success and money does not buy happiness, I can tell you it does produce certain benefits that make it worth going for anyway! Namely:

- Choices
- Goodies and services
- Something for the future
- Good feeling
- The opportunity to give back

Choices

With more money, you can choose to fulfill more of your alls. You can choose to start a business, buy a vacation home, retire earlier, go to culinary school, encourage your spouse to quit his or her job, garden, collect art, reinvest in your own company, travel, redecorate, attend all the kids' soccer games, write a novel, become a deacon in the church, participate in charities, teach, and fulfill the rest of your dreams.

Very big money gives you the independence to have almost unlimited choices: who you work for, what work you do, where you are geographically, and even the option to stop working.

Six figures is a facilitator to freedom. It's not the end, of course, but a means to an end. Our society gets too hung up on money and the conclusion that earning it is a measure of success, which is wrong. *However,* we are judged by titles and salaries, so money is important. High levels of money means freedom, and freedom means choice.

Goodies and Services

Not the least of money's benefits is that it reduces the need to worry about the basics of food, shelter, and other necessities. You can use it to live comfortably and stay out of debt.

You can also pay off student loans, secure your children's education, buy a boat (or a bigger one), get a Harley . . . or some of these goodies* with their pricey price tags:

- Joy perfume by Jean Patou: $350 for 1 ounce
- Case of Dom Perignon: $1,020
- Russian beluga caviar: $1,587 per kilo
- Metropolitan Opera, two season tickets: $3,150
- One week at the Golden Door Spa: $4,250

*Since *Forbes* magazine supplied these figures, I should add that a one-year subscription to the magazine is $57.

- Face-lift: $8,900
- Concorde round-trip from New York to London: $9,018
- Patek Philippe wristwatch: $10,800 (basic model)
- Harvard, one-year tuition, room, board, fees: $27,575
- Tennis court, clay: $45,000
- Steinway & Sons concert grand piano: $68,800
- Silver Spur Rolls-Royce: $169,900
- Maximillian Russian sable: $200,000
- Swan 68 sailing yacht: $2,292,700
- Learjet model 31A: $4.6 million
- Sikorsky S-76B helicopter: $7 million

There is no doubt that making huge money allows you to give yourself more—including more experiences. One CEO told me, "My blood pressure rose for two days. I couldn't eat, couldn't sleep in anticipation." Was it due to the pending business deal of a lifetime, an opportunity to benefit mankind and change history? I asked. "No. I got the chance to play golf with Arnold Palmer because I was the highest bidder at a celebrity auction."

Money lets you pay others to do detail and grunt work, thus freeing you to do work that makes you more money, or to engage in activities that add more fun to your life.

Then there was the self-employed seven-figure earner I called one Saturday. He said, "I'm lying in my air-conditioned hammock, reading a book, drinking iced tea, and listening to fifties music." He went on to muse about having made a lot of money: "I'm glad I was young and rich at the right time, when I could enjoy it. I don't live that way anymore. I'd be delighted to live in a small apartment and drive a pickup. Sure, I have a few bucks stashed away. But I'm down to a half dozen cars and three houses. I'm not making any money."

"Yes, you are, your company has had a record-breaking year!" I reminded him.

"Well, I don't plan to tell anybody I'm doing well," he said with a chuckle.

By the way, you might ask where he got an air-conditioned hammock. He built it himself the previous Saturday.

One of the simplest ways of making sure things get done (thus freeing up your time) is by spending money to make them happen. When you hire others to do time-consuming tasks (a housemaid, grocery shopper, driver, lawn keeper, maintenance person) things get crossed off your "do" list and you have more latitude to do what you want.

I have a friend in the oil business who made lots of money. His wife wasn't into housecleaning. He wanted the place more shipshape and he told her, suggesting she hire a maid because they could certainly afford it. She didn't want to clean their elegant domain herself, but she didn't want someone else in the house either. One day, before he left for the office, he wrote in the dust on the coffee table: DUST ME. That evening when he returned home he saw where his wife had written on the same dusty table: DO IT YOURSELF.

Although money can't buy happiness (or always get people to do what you want), it can buy things that make you feel happy in the short term. You will probably get a real thrill in buying that Lexus you've had your eye on that you weren't able to buy before.

Attorney Lawrence Land says, "When my wife and I spent a week at Norumberga Castle in Camden, Maine, it was a wonderfully happy time. But if it weren't for my income level I would never have experienced it." So it's true and it isn't necessarily true that "money doesn't buy happiness."

Something for the Future

As you make more money, theoretically you can save more, so you'll have more for the future. Having something for the future allows you to continue to have choices and get goodies.

Dr. Kelvin Kesler told me, "If you are reasonably prudent, you can have financial independence very early. Then you can feel comfortable to cut back a little on work and still maintain your style of living. With the comfort level of financial security, you decrease stress."

If you work to break into the six-figure level and you don't have savings to show for it, you're no better off than the ones who don't make it. You shouldn't have bothered working so hard if you're just going to squander it. Of all the benefits of earning money, having something for the future has to be the biggest.

"My husband and I have decided we will always live, look, and spend middle-class and avoid the temptation to upgrade or spend too freely. The exception is in our children's education," explained a $100K Club member. "We currently invest twenty-five percent of my $200K pay. We figure, with the savings, we can handle most disasters. Plus with our own money put away, others don't have a hold on us."

Many times $100K Club members have told me, "It's easier to make money than keep it." Fact is, many lose what they make.

People don't lose money because others take it from them, but because they take it from themselves. Greed, ego, sloppiness, and laziness cause loss.

With his four college buddies, a young man developed a software company. It went public, and they all became millionaires. Then the young man decided to use his profits and start another company, but on his own time. He resented having to share equity in the first venture because he felt he was the person most responsible for their success. He lost all he had made on his second business venture partially due to ego.

Overspending on good stuff obviously causes savings problems. Cartoonist Mike Shapiro draws a husband and wife talking to each other saying, "Of course we can't afford to live in this house. That's how we know we are successful."

The funny thing is, that isn't a joke in too many households.

Wanting to show people how successful you are by buying status and attention-getting stuff explains why debt is a growth business in this country. One million U.S. citizens filed for personal bankruptcy in 1996!

"Don't let your lifestyle outrun your money. To this day I could live on one-third of my salary. Therefore I'm never threatened and little variations in cash flow don't bother me. From day one I never lived close to my means, except in my first job, where everything was spent—I was only earning $650 a month. Also, people shouldn't lose perspective on the absolute value of things. I drive a twelve-year-old BMW and recently went shopping for a new one. The cost was sixty-eight thousand dollars. I couldn't bring myself to buy it although I could afford it. No car is worth that much in absolute value," says one $400K earner.

You have the option not to, but I'd recommend you live at the lowest level you can. Keep your overhead down so you're free and flexible and don't have to conform to what others want. You'll have fewer obligations to others.

Financial debt causes emotional problems, which cause physical problems, which hinder your ability to spend energy on what's necessary to make big money. It's a serious cycle to be aware of—and in control of.

Steve Binder, an investment banker with Everen Securities, advises, "Getting paid $100K is different from accumulating wealth. To accumulate wealth and go beyond having income, *save*. Save five percent off the top of your earnings starting today. In six months make it seven percent. In one year make it ten. The next six months in the new year change it to twelve. By the start of the second year make it fifteen. And always live under whatever you make, whether it is $50K or $500K."

There are four simple steps to help you have something for the future.

1. Keep expenses below income. The enjoyment of luxuries isn't worth the agony of debt. The ability to live within your means gives you contentment and peace of mind.

2. Keep a record of daily incidentals on which you spend money. You'd be surprised how much goes for candy bars, bottled water, or beer—and generally gets frittered away on incidentals. Then decide what's important to spend money on. Instead of a baby gift, offer free baby-sitting to a friend. Set aside the money you saved on incidentals and put it into a separate account. You'll be amazed how those small savings add up.

When you really want to buy something, hold off for twenty-four hours and then go look at it again. Often it doesn't look as good the second time.

3. Manage credit card use. Don't let the desire for instant gratification lure you into debt on a card. Hold off buying the latest electronic gizmo with your credit card, just because you haven't reached your credit limit yet. This is the basic self-control and discipline required of people wanting to join the $100K Club. A financial planner's recommendations:

- Use cash or checks to pay for items instead of credit cards.

- Don't go near your limit.
- Pay monthly statements in full.
- Pare down spending, then use the savings to pay off debt.
- Negotiate with your credit card company to lower interest rate or shop around for a lower-rate card.

4. Write out and stick to a personal budget.

Part of making money is managing money. That means keeping track of it. Only by keeping track can you measure it.

Remember, getting money is often by chance; keeping it is by skill. Don't get caught up on a fast track so much that it ruins your life if it stops.

A Good Feeling

"The feeling of finally succeeding at what you set out to do is like no other feeling you will ever experience," says Dennis Hoppe of Hoppe Management Concepts.

Making six figures does a lot for your self-esteem. It feels good to make a lot of money. Regardless of your motivation for making six figures, when you succeed you are pleased.

Money buys power and influence in many circles but, more important, it gives you *personal* power and freedom. Money and power feel good.

There is a mystique of wealth, called the "ultimate

magnet." The greater the money involved, the more the mystery builds, and the more attractive the person who has it. And it feels good to be attractive.

With money, all of a sudden others decide you are valuable and special. Most people like you. People with money often get more respect than those with virtue. (I'm not saying this is a good thing, just a real thing.)

Like anything good, when taken to the extreme, it can become bad. This is particularly true in the area of ego. One $100K Club member who is serving a three-year supervised-release sentence (and paid a $250K fine for fraud) was described by his probation officer: "I've never seen somebody with such a need to make themselves appear as a big shot."

Obviously, I want you to feel good about yourself, but don't get carried away with your importance.

The Opportunity to Give Back

"What I see as a major benefit of making a six-figure income is to have the opportunity to give back to my community in a way that helps others enjoy a better quality of life," says Brad Williams, president of Dakota Beverage.

John Wesley, one of the eighteenth-century founders of Methodism, said, "Make all you can, save all you can, give all you can."

But only if you make it can you give it away—to charities, social causes, friends, family. A $100K Club member in Dallas told me, "Every week I teach a free class to mothers on welfare. I like to mentor young people; invest in their future. You have to bring people along with you. That's how I give back for all I've gotten."

Owners of money have the privilege of making others happy by giving their loot away. For some $100K Club members that alone was motivation (and maybe justification) for working hard to make six-, seven-, eight-figure incomes.

THE COSTS

The cost of making six figures:

- It's never enough; you'll always want more.
- Lots of effort is required.

It's Never Enough

"The faster and more money you make, the more ways your significant other and family will find to spend it," bemoans one $100K Club member.

No matter how much you make, there is never enough; you get trapped into wanting to make more. You get accustomed to certain income levels: The more you make, the more you spend. As singer Clint Black puts it, "When you make some money, everything goes up a notch. Your whole life becomes more expensive."

Whatever you make, you'll be compelled to do it again next year. A desperation attitude can set in: "I've got to make more." Like a CEO friend of mine who was going to retire at forty to sail around the world. Forty came and went because his industry was hot and he was making more money than he ever imagined. (To his credit, at forty-seven he did sell out to one of his senior officers.) Making money is addictive. I remember a fifty-four-year-old high achiever who described his seven A.M. to seven P.M., seven-day-a-week six-figure job as being "like heroin addiction."

People tend to pinch themselves when they get to the $100K salary level. But then their goals get higher. Then it suddenly becomes $500K, then a million, and then two. As one man put it, "The temptation is to try to double and triple your income two to three more times."

You'll often hear people claim, "I'm going to make my money, then I'm out of here." It sounds good in theory, but in reality people naturally become accustomed to certain levels of loot and find that they can't accept making anything less.

Lots of Effort Is Required

Lots of effort is required to make the money and keep it coming in.

"Sometimes I'm afraid of just running out of energy. Some days I just want to stay in bed. My calendar looks like a snowstorm. Every day I have to have breakfast with employees, lunch with a customer, and dinner with a supplier," said a senior vice president of a computer company.

The irony is, you start out in the eight-hour-a-day jobs and work hard to become the boss, then get to work the *twelve*-hour-a-day jobs. In the extreme you can get totally burned out, totally tired, and ruined for anything else.

The list is endless in terms of what is required as you move up in a corporation or move out into your own enterprise. In addition to doing the work at hand to get a product or service into the paying hands of a customer, your time in high-paying jobs will be consumed in:

- Juggling priorities
- Managing and supervising relationships among people
- Delegating and facilitating across functions and organizations
- Cheering on others
- Building egos
- Coaching, counseling, teaching, guiding, and influencing co-workers, financiers, customers, the

public, the media, and even your family and friends
- Making policy, developing missions, strategic planning, organizing and focusing
- Making decisions with limited information
- Speaking in public, speaking in meetings, speaking incessantly on the phone
- Traveling places you don't want to go

Malcolm Forbes wrote, "By the time we've made it, we've had it." I know of more than one top person who opted for surgery just to have an excuse for a vacation.

Since we know making $100K will take a lot of effort, find something you like to do. Do work you love and enjoy—otherwise it won't matter how much you make. Good things do come to people who work long, hard hours in something that fits their alls.

How Can You Avoid Paying a High Price?

Understanding the potential downside of making big money is the first step to avoid paying the price. When you recognize the possibility and choose to do something about it, you'll likely succeed.

Always wanting more and never having enough isn't inherently a bad thing. If your motivation is a money-grubbing, greedy, hoarding, keep-from-others perspective, you'll be paying a much bigger price than I've laid out here. But wanting more so you can save for future disasters, provide for children's college education, care for aging parents, have retirement security, and give to philanthropic causes . . . well, always wanting more is *not* a bad thing.

Today (not some nebulous time in the future when you have made the big bucks, but now, while you're still working on it) lay out a systematic plan for the total sum of money you are willing to allocate for a particular purpose over a time period. Plan in advance what you'll need for living.

Don't file this itemized summary away. Keep it handy to review *before* you sign the papers for the new automobile, bigger mortgage, sailboat, or Neiman Marcus credit card. Live lean. Now, and in the future.

Lean does not mean Scrooge-like frugal. It means well below your means. There are far too many real-life stories of people who work hard all their lives scrimping, saving, and delaying all gratification until retirement. Then, within one year, they die.

Remember the second chapter on balancing your alls? That has to happen both when you are with money and without.

Bottom line: Always wanting more is usually keeping up with the Joneses as opposed to satisfying needs. Control yourself. If you can't control the money you earn and are unable to stay out of debt, don't waste the time and effort going for a big financial goal.

Lots of effort is required in making a six-figure income. That is true. But effort isn't just expended toward working hard. Effort is needed to maintain the balance throughout your journey. Effort is required to avoid debt. Effort is required in maintaining healthy friendships. Life *is* effort.

Money is necessary. It doesn't make for happiness, but it does make life's other problems easier to deal with. As a $100K Club member, you will have the same problems as anyone else. You'll just have them in a bigger house!

Let me summarize the pros and cons of making big bucks as $100K Club members have experienced it.

First the cons:

- Fear in keeping
- Temptation in using
- Guilt in abusing
- Sorrow in losing
- Too obsessed with business; forget leisure, solitude, and thought
- Doesn't keep you from getting sick
- Others think your money is some part of public trust
- Causes you to get soft

Now the pros:

- As Ben Franklin said, money begets money
- Gives you lawful pleasures

- It's a nice surprise for yourself
- Gives you power for good
- Leisure
- Liberty
- Get to learn how to dispense with it
- Avoids inconvenience and discomfort of poverty
- Minimizes idleness
- Makes you stand upright and proud
- Easier to conceal wealth than poverty
- You can cease to think about needs since they are satisfied
- Can wear it, share it, use it
- Makes people around you happy

As you can see, the cost of getting into the $100K Club is low—or at least manageable. Whereas the benefits are high and really unlimited.

To help you enjoy the advantages and minimize costs, here are Ten Canons of $100K Club members:

1. Set a big, bold goal—say, $100K by age thirty-three.
2. School yourself in the ways others have made it.
3. Take risks within an inch of your career life.
4. Have better tools than anybody else.
5. Focus on your goal but get support from those close to you. Assign them to keep you focused on personal growth, not just the dollar signs.
6. Stay debt-free. Keep overhead low.
7. Have a good time, even when you're doing intense stuff.

8. Avoid naysayers.
9. Share the personal growth and benefits you're experiencing with those who are supporting you.
10. Set a good example for others to follow in the future.

After reading this book, you know what is required to make $100K. You know the steps to take and the steps to avoid. You know what you will gain, and you know what you need to refrain from losing. You've read firsthand what those who are already there think you need to do to get there yourself.

Now you need to *test* yourself. Use the final chapter, "The $100K Creed," to honestly evaluate yourself now and find out what you need to be doing in the future to get to $100K and beyond.

"I remember certain former *employees who were obsessed with achieving a certain level of six-figure compensation. Obsessed to the detriment of their ability to be productive or to function effectively with others. Unfortunately, including an effective relationship with their immediate family. I think that is a sure waste of one's self."*

—JIM BIUNDO,
President, US West
Investment Management
Company

"If someone were to draw a caricature of you, it should have big eyes and ears. Listen and watch extensively. Learn from others' success and failures. And always listen and watch yourself as well. Your own actions and results will provide wonderful lessons. Finally, never change this posture, whether you're making $50K or exceeding $100K. Remember, as it has been said, success is a journey, not a destination."

—GEOFF PIKE,
Director, F-O-R-T-U-N-E
Personnel Consultants

THE $100,000 CLUB

> *"Develop people; raise their expectations; establish a set of core values; persist in continuous improvement."*
>
> —LARRY HALL,
> President, KN Energy

CHAPTER 8

The $100K Creed

I've laid out what it takes for you to get into the $100K Club. In this final chapter I'm providing a twenty-point test for you to take (and use as a guideline) to *guarantee* your admittance.

It will be easy for you to test your success potential: For every statement you can—with a clear conscience—check off, you are one step closer. You'll find that twenty *achievable* steps aren't too difficult to get you to $100K.

The $100K Creed

☐ I accept the fact that it is okay to set a high financial goal—so I've set a big one. I'm aware of where my attitude toward money comes from and I'm in control of my perspective toward money today. I accept: I can make big money. This can be done by me. And

I'm willing to take on the responsibility necessary. My timetable for making six figures is _________.

- ☐ I do something specific to add to my self-worth every day: learn a new job skill, develop a new personality trait, solve a time-consuming energy-draining problem, control time, manage an attitude, improve appearances, build muscle. Every day I can point to something new I've learned, regardless of how small.

- ☐ First and foremost, I do good work in the job I'm paid to do. Good work by the company's standards, not just my own. I can quantify the 10 percent extra I always do, offering my boss more than just sitting at my desk. I regularly do more than what's necessary, then keep doing it. And I let the right people know about my contributions on a regular basis without overdoing it.

- ☐ I work in a profit center and understand how my job fits into the big picture. I work in a job function (or am preparing to move into one) in which six-figure salaries can occur.

- ☐ *I've determined my alls.* I've written them down, and I follow them. They are: (list). I take four minutes (at least) every day for every one of my alls.

- ☐ I accept the fact of office politics, understand it is part of my job, and try to work effectively within the game. I understand and follow the company line, as long as it's legal, ethical, and moral behavior. I accept the seemingly unacceptable; in other words, I've learned to live with an imperfect business world.

☐ I'm becoming an expert in ____. My expert status is needed and valued in the company where I work. I plan targets, steps, and measurements toward this and I think each out, clear through a deadline. I initiate quarterly meetings with my manager to check progress. If I'm self-employed, I initiate the same progress reports with customers.

☐ I go out of my way to meet people to build personal and professional networks outside my company and industry. Every day of the workweek I initiate a "keep in touch" call with someone in my circle of business friends/contacts. Once a week a handwritten note of congratulations, praise, consolation, or notification goes into the mail from me to an old (or new) contact. Every month I can point to something specific I've done to put my name in front of the business public, and specifically executive recruiters. (If self-employed, that might mean contact with the media instead of recruiters.)

☐ I deliver what I promise. I try to be a person of substance: genuinely good and happy. I keep a healthy level of fun going at all times. I have a good time while doing intense stuff.

- ☐ I regularly take huge risks (within an inch of my career life) and am not afraid to fail. I'm willing to take on the responsibility of being a leader. I make decisions when needed. I'm not afraid to make decisions that could result in mistakes. I'm the first to recognize and admit my mistakes. And I avoid repeating them.

- ☐ When I want to give up, I don't. Period. When others encourage me to give up, I don't. Period. (I do give up when the facts point to it being a good idea.)

- ☐ Intellectual curiosity runs rampant in my thinking and action. I'm full of questions. I ask questions for clarification to avoid assumption, and to learn something new, never to put people into a corner. I don't assume *anything.* I ask. When I question, I ask three times in different ways to get people thinking and to enable me to learn more about what they do and do not know.

- ☐ I avoid busywork, or activities that derail me. I don't waste time. I constantly try to eliminate excuses.

- ☐ When I open my mouth, I always try to be as straightforward and clear-speaking as possible. Before I open my mouth, I silently think through what I'm going to say, anticipate the reaction, and alter my words for the effect I want. I judiciously hold my tongue; I don't express every thought that comes to mind. (I know I may need to eat my words later and they won't taste very good.)

- ☐ When there is a choice to do something marginally dishonest or unethical, I don't take it. (Even though no one else knows.)

- ☐ I intelligently observe others, in any situation, and try to choose something different than they do (without being weird).

- ☐ I anticipate objections and rejection and prepare ways to handle them in advance. I don't accept "no" without really testing what kind of "no" it means. Rejection doesn't faze me.

- ☐ I live below my means. I keep out of debt. I save for the future.

- ☐ I focus on my goal but support those around me to help them reach their financial and career goals.

- ☐ I enjoy myself and the money I earn while minimizing the costs of making money.

You will notice this checklist does not include anything unrealistic or that is not doable. I'm not asking you to get three master's degrees, bench press 250 pounds, or dye your hair blond.

To increase your chances for financial success, simply work on the items *not* marked. Those are the areas that will separate you from the competition. (The competition being yourself!) With each additional bit of effort, and subsequent item checked off, you get closer to your goal.

If you do 100 percent on this list and are not getting $100K, call me. We need to talk! Because if you decide on what you want and put everything you have into it, I guarantee you'll get it.

Of course, I fully understand that striving to make big money is not always psychologically, politically, or socially correct. But can you really afford to wait for the world's approval? No, you can't—and you shouldn't. Don't ever succumb to any naysayers. Just because they can't or won't go for the brass ring doesn't mean you can't.

Enthusiasm and energy keeps you motivated and going, but it is competence and skill that keeps you winning. We all cross the finish line; the winners just find a better way to get there.

From this book you can see the way the $100K Club members do it—now it's up to you to *work* it. And there will never be a better time for you to work it than *now.*

"If I were writing the laws, I'd make it a crime to give up on yourself—because it certainly carries a life sentence if you do."

—D. A. Benton

Acknowledgments

Thanks to these individuals who gave their time and opinions on how to make $100K:

Dr. Stephen Albert
Nancy Albertini
Lee and Mary Alexander
Scott Ball
Reuben Ballye
Lucy Baney
Daniel Beer
Bob Berkowitz
John Bianchi
Steve Binder
Jim Biundo
Dorothy Bland
Lynn Butkus
Jack Callahan
Ada Chen
Michael Christman
Joe Coca
Mindy Credi
Gayle Crowell
Jeff Cunningham
Souman Das
Tony Donofrio
Dan Dornan
John and Sandra Downing
Gary Erb
Bill Fairfield
Jack Falvey
Michelle and Jim Fitzhenry

Art Fossum
Dave Fults
Rich Gartrell
Neil Georgi
Don Goings
Liza Graves
Mike Hirshorn
Dennis Hoppe
Ernie Howell
Richard Jacobs
J. M. Jones
Gordon and Janice Kai
Linda Kelleher
Liz Kennedy
Dr. Kelvin Kesler
John Krebbs
Karna Kruckenburg-Schofer
Ken Kunze
Lawrence Land
Judy Laxineta
Jack Linkletter
Peter and Cathy Mackins
Reuben Mark
Clif May
Jim McBride
Art McDaniels
Jim Mead
Steve Milovich
Lauren Nelson
John and Barbara Odeggard
Art Oldham
Walter Olkewicz
Kip Oram
Stan Payne
Geoff Pike
Brian Piper
Katy Pitrowski
Rich Post
Dave Powelson
Bob Price
Judy Priola
Marcia Pryde
Gail Robinson
Ken Roper
Carolyn Rose
Mike Rosser

Al Royce
Sam Sanderson
Joyce Scott
Mike Scott
Paul Schlossberg
Dick Schmer
Steve Sekiguchi
Ernie Sewall
Fred Starr
Hugh Sullivan
Jack Southard
E. A. "Butch" Teppe
Larry Thede
Brad Thomas
Bina Thompson
Richard Torrenzano
Sol Trujillo
Marilyn Vines
John Wager
Rod Wailes
Don Wass
Craig Watson
Mark Wheless
Dennis Wu

Index

INDEX

INDEX